GOOD MORNING DETROIT
THE KELLY & CO. STORY

BY JOHN KELLY
AND MARILYN TURNER

WITH LINDA BENSON

CONTEMPORARY
BOOKS, INC.
CHICAGO ▪ NEW YORK

Library of Congress Cataloging-in-Publication Data

Kelly, John, 1927–
  Good morning Detroit.

  1. Kelly & Co. (Television program)
2. Kelly, John, 1927–   3. Turner, Marilyn.
4. Television personalities—Michigan—Detroit—
Biography. I. Turner, Marilyn. II. Title.
PN1992.77.K453K4   1986   791.45′72   86-19789
ISBN 0-8092-5093-4

Copyright © 1986 by John Kelly and Marilyn Turner
All rights reserved
Published by Contemporary Books, Inc.
180 North Michigan Avenue, Chicago, Illinois 60601
Manufactured in the United States of America
Library of Congress Catalog Card Number: 86-19789
International Standard Book Number: 0-8092-5093-4

Published simultaneously in Canada by Beaverbooks, Ltd.
195 Allstate Parkway, Valleywood Business Park
Markham, Ontario L3R 4T8 Canada

CONTENTS

To my most marvelous mother and father, who never tried to steer me into a career of their choosing, and who have always given unqualified and loving support.

—John

To Carm and Eve, who always wanted the best for me, who sowed the seeds of success early and well.

To Carm, who thought "his little girl" was the greatest and never missed a "Kelly & Company" until he died November 19, 1984.

To Eve, who still watches us every day.

Thank you, Dad. Thank you, Mom.

—Marilyn

ACKNOWLEDGMENTS

JOHN

There have been so many people at so many stations in so many cities who all led to "Kelly & Company," it would be impossible to include them in this book without making it resemble a telephone directory. Nevertheless, they all played a hand in shaping the career that brought me to this point. For example, there's Wayne "Profit" Crib who gave me my first job at KHMO in Hannibal, Missouri; Joe Higgins, who fired me from my last job in management; and Bob McBride, the man with the faith to bring this guy from Peoria to Detroit. Just a few of the many from KHMO, WTAR-TV, WTVO, WJIM-TV, WLWA, WMBD-TV, WJKB-TV, and especially WXYZ-TV—they were (and are) writers, directors, producers, stage managers, department heads, graphic artists, photographers, set designers, cameramen and women, technical directors, projectionists, editors, engineers, reporters, account executives, and managers; artisans and artists all, all contributed to this book in some fashion. Good old Mason Weaver, whom I tease mercilessly about "yesterday's newsreel," who has done us all from Soupy to the Lady of Charm to a sometimes charmless me, for the hours in the control room calling those shots . . . and to Chuck and Art, our stage bosses. And our stagehands, the most creative bunch I have ever worked with—anywhere. And then, Ellen Kennedy Stepian, one-time producer and all-time friend, who came to our rescue at the last minute.

And our editor, Kyle Roggenbuck, who deserves an award for all-time patience.

I thank you. Boy, do I thank you!

MARILYN

There are countless dozens of people who touch us as we move through our careers—people who at the time (we think then) provide a negative aspect, and others who just plain go out of their way to help. Many names you forget; many you remember. For instance, a guy I remember only as Bill, who picked me out of a hundred other contestants to do commercials at CFPL-TV in London, Ontario, thus starting my television career. I *never* seemed to please him, but I learned.

And the management of WJBK-TV, who took the chance with an unknown little Canadian girl, starting her doing weather when she knew provinces better than states. Phil Nye, news director of WXYZ-TV, who believed I was good enough to do the weather "across the board." Bob Woodruff, who was sure I had what it took to do a talk show. And all of those producers whom I have worked with these last nine years: Dan Weaver, Randy Barone, Nancy Lenzen, Synka Curtis, Jill Coughlin, Barb Koster, Brad Hurtado, Lisa Fisco, Dianne Hudson, and Carnell Sessoms. We are family, and I love them. We've had fun times and sad times, and we've shared. Floor managers and directors. My two sons, Rob and Dean, who had to learn it wasn't always great to have a mom who was a "local celeb." To Lulu Refugee, our housekeeper of fifteen years, and Dani Jacobson—I couldn't survive without them. Ellen Kennedy, who at the eleventh hour, answered the call. As she would say, God love ya . . . thanks, thanks, thanks.

1
GOOD MORNING, DETROIT

JOHN

My arms flail, and I kick out, struggling to be free. Something is holding me down and who the hell is screaming at me? With a desperate heave my legs are loosened and I swing to my feet, swaying, looking around wildly in the darkened room. In a moment I lurch to the foot of the bed, reaching madly for the nearby dresser top. The shouting stops. I have turned the clock-radio off.

It's 4:15 A.M. My mouth tastes like the bottom of a bird cage looks. My left knee, kicked by a horse many years ago, aches dully, and there's a small pain at the base of my spine. In the bathroom, I raise my head from the basin to dry my face and note that my hair appears as if there was an attempt to screw my skull into the headboard overnight. I switch off the light, wait to adjust to the darkness again, and tiptoe out, noting the dogs who do not move and a wife who is doing a good impression of the dogs.

In the kitchen, I put coffee on, slice melon, and get my toast ready. I go back to the bedroom to coax the dogs out. We descend fourteen floors and head for an area cunningly known as the "poodle path." It is dark outside. At 4:30 A.M. it is always dark outside, regardless of the season. The doberman sniffs suspiciously at the grass because it may be damp. She doesn't like to get her feet wet, hates snow, and refuses to go out in the rain at all. The poodle is racing in joyful circles with occasional stops to sniff and take care of other things. Shortly we are back upstairs and I begin my breakfast, sharing portions with the dogs and starting the homework for today's "Kelly & Company." Through it all, I keep an eye on the clock. In a little over four hours, we'll be on the air. Soon it's a quarter past five, and time for Marilyn. It's so easy to awaken her. She's invariably pleasant and soft-voiced. Why can't I be like that?

MARILYN

It was obvious early in our marriage that John is a bear for the first half-hour or so that he is awake. He's snappish and grumpy and would rather not talk. But he does make good coffee. So our routine works well for us. He is also a clock-watcher. This man is on time for dinner reservations, airline flights, appointments, dates with friends, you name it. If there is a time to be set and a time to be met, John Kelly will meet the challenge! He drives me crazy sometimes. *He* says it's because of all those years of television and radio where timing is so crucial, and I'm sure that's true. But it *is* irritating. I am not that rigid.

2

So it's right at a quarter past five that he gets me up, and—bless him—makes sure that I'm awake, and then he leaves me alone. A quick brush of the hair and into the same robe and slippers I've been using since our show began, I think. After a while I join him at the kitchen table, and then I begin to appreciate him. It *is* nice to have your melon sliced (sometimes even melon balls) and coffee ready to go (even if it is stronger than I like it). All I have to do is open my homework and get at it.

The "homework" is all of the material assembled by our producers for the day's show. We already have a general idea of the content, of course. We've seen the names of the various guests scheduled and posted on a bulletin board in our office. It lists all the guests who are booked for the upcoming three weeks along with a brief note about their book or movie. We've discussed it in a meeting the previous day, and usually that's followed by a series of individual talks with a producer/researcher as the day goes on. But this early morning time is when we really get into the details.

There are mornings sitting there when I think, "My God, not *another* show involving sex." I know there is interest, but we do get complaints even though ratings inch up. But there are those days I hope we can just go a month without a show involving sex.

Usually it's pretty quiet at the table. I mean, he's buried in his notes, and so am I. John relies more on his memory and recall, probably because of his days in news. I like to make notes, lots of them. Occasionally I'll think I don't like the division—the way the program is divided between us. Or maybe I'd rather not do a certain thing. John will agree, and we'll change it right there. The producers may be a little upset but they go along, of course, and for the most part it works out.

By half past five or a quarter to six, John is stuffing his material into a briefcase and heading for the shower.

JOHN

I like to get to the office by half past six. That gives me time to read a couple of papers, talk with the stagehands while they are drinking their coffee, and generally get the feel of the day's show. It takes me about forty-five minutes to get ready to leave the house. The shave and the shampoo and the shower go quickly. Then I dress in casual clothes and pull out the suits, shirts, ties, and socks for the two shows we did until recently. Now it's only one suit, so the load I carry is smaller. But for four years I must have looked like a pack horse when I headed for my car with my briefcase over one shoulder, a bag of shirts and shoes over the other, and suit hangers hooked over a couple of fingers. I couldn't bend over without dropping something.

MARILYN

The one time I *do* watch the clock is early in the morning. Ten past seven is a key time. Our apartment building has valet parking, thank God, and ten past seven is the time I call down for the car. In the meantime, it's my bath, and every other day I wash my hair. For several years now we have had the services of a hairdresser and makeup artist, and it's wonderful! Before that I did my own—that really took extra time. Now I just blow dry my hair, pull on a jumpsuit, and leave home. Oh, sometimes I carry extra baggage, but usually the jumpsuit is the routine. John says his office is his office but my office is my closet. And it's true. All of my clothing and jewelry and accessories are there. There's even a makeup chair. Any meetings we need to hold are in John's office, because that's the only place there is room!

JOHN

People always gasp when they learn the hours we have to keep, but it's just as bad for the producers. On the average, they're in the office for ten hours a day. At home hardly a night passes for them without time on the phone checking on guests, last-minute changes, and other routine emergencies! Occasionally they even meet a plane so that an uncertain celebrity won't wind up lost or in the wrong hotel. That has happened. When you can't find your main guest an hour before the show, it tends to mess up your day. So between seven and half past seven the producers arrive. There's some wake-up chatter and newspaper checking in case there is a story we can use in a later show. Soon the floor manager and director have arrived. We gather and go over the entire show in detail. The floor manager has back-timed so we'll be on the nose from beginning to end with commercials, announcements, and the varying lengths of segments assigned to guests and subjects.

MARILYN

Worrywart John will keep at it, but by eight each morning I've *got* to be ready for makeup and hair. If there's one memory of "Kelly & Company" I'll probably carry to the grave, it will be of me, flat on my back in a makeup chair, the artist bent over my face and one or two producers standing over me discussing and informing while the director and stage manager wander in and out with things they consider important. Our secretary may have a reminder of an appointment later in the day, and at some point John pokes his head in wondering if they're ready for *his* makeup. By this time he's dressed for the show, and already on his high. Then I'm out of the makeup chair and at my desk. The hairdresser is working on me while I'm looking at my notes again. It's about twenty minutes to nine. John has popped into the makeup chair, and he's doing one-liners while makeup and hair are making suggestions to me for jewelry and clothing. Now, John *is* funny. There are times when he can make anyone hysterical with laughter, me included. At this hour, however, I do not consider him a barrel of laughs, and I suggest that he shut up. That's *my* tension talking; he knows that, and I know he knows that.

JOHN

By a quarter to nine one of the producers, usually Jill Coughlin, is in the studio talking to the audience. She kids them about applause, about speaking up and taking part; then at ten to nine, she introduces me. It's time for the warm-up, part two. And it's important. We loosen up the audience, get them laughing and talking and applauding. A great deal of what I do is ad-lib, a lot of it is routine. All of it is designed to gauge the crowd, let them know we like them and we need them. Then, with about two minutes to go, I introduce Marilyn. They just love her. And then we're on the air. One way or another, for one *reason* or another, we *prove* it's a live show. The viewers may not know it, because they shouldn't have to know about the problems that can develop, but we know it by the way all of us—producers, director, stage manager, engineers, and Marilyn and I—are wrung out by a quarter to eleven. As Richard Simmons once told an audience here, ". . . 'Kelly & Company' is L-I-V-E!"

For instance, June 13, 1986.

Friday the 13th, of course.

What a show we thought we had. Anthony Perkins is here to plug his new film, *Psycho III*. Gayle Rivers, the nom de plume of a Viet Nam veteran—former mercenary, counter-terrorist for hire to any western government, assassin—is here as author of a book on how he would control terrorism. Famous attorney Alan Dershowitz will talk about how he got Klaus von Bulow acquitted of attempted murder charges, and we also have the queen of chocolate chip cookies, Mrs. Fields.

What a show.

The schedule was to start with Gayle Rivers, two segments with John; Anthony Perkins, two segments with Marilyn; then our famous Kelly's Quiz, with John; Mrs. Fields and her cookies for one segment with John; and closing out with Dershowitz and Marilyn for two segments. Good balance and separation of the heavy and lighter stuff—at least, that was the plan.

MARILYN

We're already a little tense because Anthony Perkins's public relations people had insisted that the interviewer see the Perkins film before going on the air with him. With our schedule, it was just impos-

7

sible. John and I simply had no time for any activity aside from the job and a night's rest during the week. So we quietly arranged for the producer of the Perkins segment to see the film the night before, and give me a complete briefing on it before the show; we were certain it would work out. It did, but there was a small kink in the plan.

JOHN

The show began, as planned, with Gayle Rivers. He was disguised. He wore a wig, false glasses, and I was sure he had some padding in his cheeks. He slumped in his chair, which a military man simply would not do. In addition, we shot him in silhouette. Under questioning, we talked of his earlier activities: a rescue mission in Lebanon in which many were killed, clandestine missions for our government and others, and what Rivers and others like him felt should be done to counter international terrorism. The audience was enthralled and asked many questions. He told them simply that we should adopt the terrorists' methods and act, not react; find terrorists and eliminate them, before they did more. He was applauded as we went to commercials, and applauded again as he left the studio.

I felt good. It had gone well and now it was time for Anthony Perkins.

No, it wasn't. I was met at the studio door with about a minute left in the break. Perkins was late, and we were flipping the schedule. Mrs. Fields was next, and I was the interviewer. Now, this sounds simple, but it can cause consternation in a control room. An entire series of visuals had been programmed into various electronic machines, based on the schedule. The visuals had to be shuffled and adjusted with lightning speed while I adjusted my own thinking and Mrs. Fields rushed through makeup. Of course, we did it. And it went well. Mrs. Fields, a beautiful woman of about thirty years, has cookie stores all over the world. Her answers were routine, with one exception. I asked her if getting her business started was made more difficult because she was not only a woman, but a good-looking woman. She gazed at me for a long moment and then said yes, it had been. She found that people tended not to look past her surface beauty to find a brain and good business sense. It was heartfelt and honest. The audience liked her at first, then loved her when they heard all would sample Mrs. Fields cookies later in the show.

MARILYN

Anthony Perkins arrived shortly after John began the segment with the cookie lady. I was told by a quaking intern that Perkins was upset. He'd just left a radio show where it was discovered that the interviewer had *not* seen the movie, and that had not been the plan. Of course, neither had I. Now, sometimes I'm excited or even nervous when a star I have known of and seen for years is on our show. But this time—for whatever reason—I was calm and confident. And if he doesn't like what I do, I thought, "the hell with him." He would get publicity for his movie, and that was what it was all about.

On the air, I introduced him; Perkins did what we call a "walk-on," meaning he entered from the wings, to thunderous applause. We shook hands, he sat down, and the first thing out of my mouth was, "I think I'm afraid of you!" I learned later that he was somewhat taken aback by that. But it seemed to get

us off on the right foot. He was dressed in nonde-
script trousers, a brown leather jacket, dress shirt
with a bolo tie (those cowboy things), and running
shoes. Very tall and almost skinny. We discussed the
film and all the *Psycho* films—three of them. At one
point we ran a clip from an earlier show when Janet
Leigh told John that she still never takes a shower!
He chuckled at that and talked about Janet briefly.
We looked at a clip from the movie and discussed
that scene. Later, the audience was filled with questions for him, questions about his career, admiring
comments about all of his work as well as the *Psycho*
films and others. My personal favorite, however, was
the lady who stood up and said, "Mr. Perkins, did
you know your socks don't match?" Without a pause
or turning a hair, he replied, "Well, I just took
whatever was on top this morning."

Anthony Perkins has a marvelous face: expressive,
handsome in a different way, very photogenic, as
they used to say in Hollywood. I caught a sneaky
look at the monitor, and the director thought so, too,
as he kept Perkins in close-ups. It was soon over.
During the commercial break I told him good-bye.
Mr. Perkins smiled, waved at the audience, and left.
He never suspected I had not seen the movie—and to
tell the truth, I felt like I had! Sorry, Tony.

JOHN

Alan Dershowitz was excellent, and Marilyn—fascinated with the Klaus von Bulow case and the story of
the super rich—was perfect. With her gentle
prompting—not that he needed much because all
trial lawyers love to talk, I've noticed—he spoke of a
mysterious dope peddler, his dozens of law students
who did research on the case, the lives of those

people, and how he won the case. She did a good job.

MARILYN

As soon as we finish the show, at half past ten, we thank our audience for being there—and John tells them they can't leave. Actually, every day we record promotional announcements for the next day's show, and we do it with the studio audience. So we're not out of the studio until about a quarter to eleven.

JOHN

At this time we have a postproduction meeting. This particular Friday the 13th was filled with reviewing the gentle and necessary deception involving Anthony Perkins as well as the ways we got through the last-minute change without any major problems in the control room, tape room, and studio. Theoretically, the postproduction meeting is where we work out problems encountered on that day's show and make great plans. But on *this* day, the truth is that though it was not yet noon we had been going for seven hours, and we were drained.

MARILYN

I've always called it the sinking spell. The adrenaline drains away and, for a time, you're feeling exhausted. One evening recently John looked at me and wondered aloud how a man who couldn't wait to get into management and a woman who wanted some money to help get her husband through medical school wound up doing what we do, and doing it with each other.

2
EARLY GEOGRAPHY: NORTH, SOUTH, EAST, MIDWEST

❖

JOHN

For twenty-one years my professional and personal fortunes have been tied to the city of Detroit. In broadcasting, and in the world of television broadcasting in particular, that is a long time. Long enough to call it home? Probably. It certainly feels like home. I say that for reasons that are hard to define, except that there have been times in my life when I have lived elsewhere and found myself longing for the Midwest, its pace, its attitudes, its rhythms, even the cadences of its speech patterns.

My earliest years were spent in St. Louis. South St. Louis was the name of the neighborhood, and it was heavy on immigrants: many German immigrants, some of whom were straight from the old country; a substantial number of Jewish immigrants; and a sprinkling of Irish, which was my family heritage.

Some of my earliest memories are of the smells in the four-family flat that we lived in—the Jewish cooking on Fridays, and the German cooking all the rest of the days of the week.

In those days, in that kind of neighborhood, we had an extended family of aunts, uncles, and grand-parents on both sides. My parents were Irish-American, and in the kind of ethnic neighborhood I grew up in, that said a lot about you. My mother was the one who passed on the pride of the Irish. She kept track of the Kellys, the Kelins, the Dardens, and the O'Neals who made up our ancestry. My dad, when he spoke of it at all, told stories only of the relatives who had settled off to the "west," and gone bad. He told great tales of a horse thief in Oklahoma, of a wild "black" Irishman who was caught and hanged.

It didn't matter so much whether you were Irish Protestant or Irish Catholic in my neighborhood. You were poor either way, and we were poor Irish in those years. When you are a kid, though, you don't know you're poor. "Poor" is a condition that happens to somebody else, and I was too young to know the difference anyhow. It was only years later that I learned that during the Depression years, my mother, father, and I lived on fifty cents a day for a long time.

When he was a boy, my dad worked as a rusher between two St. Louis movie houses, the Princess and the Cinderella. When a film finished showing in one movie house, he would take it, hop on a street-car, and go across town with it to the other. Later, to help make ends meet, he played the clarinet in a band on weekends, and also was an aspiring Shake-spearean actor in amateur productions around the city. I guess that's where I got my theatrical bent.

Dad met Mother in high school, Cleveland High,

which I attended twenty years later. They married and both went to work. For a time they worked at the Brown Shoe Company. My mother still relishes telling the story of the real brawl my dad got into with a factory bully. As these things go, the story has no doubt become romantically embellished over the years. It seems the guy insulted my mother, and my good old Irish father cleaned his clock. Of course it may have been a mutual cleaning, but Sir John did indeed fight for his lady's honor.

Later, my dad got a job with the Federated Metals Company, one of the big foundries that made up an important part of the industrial base in St. Louis, and which became a division of the American Smelting and Refining Company. He rose up through the ranks to a management position in Chicago, and took an early retirement.

My dad is now eighty-three years old and given to recollections. He recalls my mother and what a strong woman she was. For most city homes in those days, particularly in St. Louis with its close proximity to Illinois mines, coal was the most common fuel for heating. The coal was delivered by truck, dumped in the street at the curb, and the coal man, with shovel and wheelbarrow, transferred the coal to your coal bin. He would fill his wheelbarrow, pick it up, and wheel it down the gangway toward the rear of the house. So one cold winter day when things were *really* tight, Mom bypassed the coal man and spent the entire day filling buckets and carrying them back to the coal chute and dumping it in. She moved an entire ton of coal that day, and saved fifty cents. She was exhausted, and my father was astounded.

My mother was born Selma Ethyl Darden. As far as I know, she's never been too happy being an Ethyl. On the other hand, her mother was named

Della, and I don't think she would be too happy with that either! She never worked outside the home while raising us kids—the house was her domain. Dad's efforts took care of his family, and she took care of the house and her sons, which was more than enough work. Dad always said he had the better deal.

Mom is a southerner by birth and inclination. When I was a boy she always told me about one of her Darden ancestors who was the fattest man in the world. We kids were somewhat skeptical, but recently I found his name, Mills Darden, in the *Guinness Book of World Records*. At seven feet six inches tall, Mills Darden weighed in at 1,020 pounds and lived from 1798 to 1857. How's that for a claim to fame?

While Dad was working his way up the ranks at Federated Metals, he traveled quite a bit. He'd go away for a day or two or more every two or three weeks. Some of my earliest memories are of all of us piling into the family car, a 1934 Chevrolet four-door black sedan, and taking him to Union Station. It wasn't to see him off; it was because we had to have the car to get around while he was gone and Mom wasn't about to pay a sitter. As a matter of fact, we didn't even know what a baby-sitter was.

I have two brothers. I am oldest. Five years younger is Dan, or to be precise, Daniel Allen. Dan is now a minister in Vermont. The youngest is Kenneth Lee. Ken lives near Phoenix, Arizona, and after a series of setbacks, is established in a business and is studying for the ministry, rather late in life. Each of my brothers has four children. I have three. Marilyn sometimes has difficulty understanding my relationship with my family—she being an only child. While my family is far-flung, I know and they know that one cry for help means a brother will be on the way to do what he can, as much as he can, as quickly as he can.

But it wasn't always that way. When you're a big brother, little brothers are a pain in the ass. Especially when you're five years older, as I was. The little guys, particularly Dan, the red-headed middle brother, always wanted to tag along. I, of course, did not wish his company *at all.* I would proceed on my way with him following about ten or fifteen feet behind me, pleading to be included. Thinking back on it, I can picture myself heading down the street, all of ten years old or so, with this ragged baseball mitt my uncle had given me (leftover from *his* boyhood) and maybe a baseball, too, going toward a vacant lot where the guys were getting a game together, and yelling at this little guy tagging along behind me. I even used to throw things like rocks and stones at him, trying to scare him off. Carefully though, so I wouldn't hit him. Now, it seems hard to believe, but I guess that's the way kids are. Or at least how I was.

When I was small, I remember things called Big Little Books. They were the predecessors of comic books. Instead of a page full of comic strips, they were small and fat, designed for only one cartoon panel on a page. The covers were heavy cardboard, and they were about an inch and a half thick and about four inches square. Once I was heading up the steps to the room my brothers and I shared to read the brand new one I had bought with grass cutting money, and Dan was following, as usual, and begging to get at the book. In a rage, I turned and threw it. The throw was off, and it him in the nose, making it bleed. To my shame, I lied to my mother and

17

blamed it on my youngest brother, Kenny. Until I confessed to them all about five years ago, they all believed that Ken had done it, including Ken himself! The power of suggestion, I guess.

Kenny was the family tightwad. It was a family joke, of course, but he *was* a little near with a buck. At one point, he carried a coin-changer on his belt. Those were the things with four upright tubes attached to each other which hung on a belt at your waist. Each tube was a different size to carry quarters, dimes, nickels, and pennies. There was a small lever that you jiggled with your thumb, lifting the coins out of a slot, one by one. Bus and streetcar conductors and paperboys had them then. And Kenny. When he was small, it was his delight to lever change for Mother and Dad, but *never* for Dan or me. Ken saved enough to have his first car earlier than any of us. It's funny how life turns. He wound up dead broke, divorced, and out of work at age forty. However, he slowly fought his way back.

Performing was something that was an early—and natural—part of my formative years. I remember being in charge of taking Kenneth, who had a speech impediment, on the streetcar a couple of times a week to a speech correction specialist across town. I'd sit and wait for him during his lesson and bring him back home. As a young teenager, I considered it boring and tedious, but some of the pear-shaped tones must have rubbed off. Furthermore, I charmed the speech correction specialist, Mrs. Tucker, who got me involved in performing in amateur theatricals. My first role came about when Mrs. Tucker needed a Boy Scout and I fit the bill. She saw I had possibilities, and I did several juvenile roles with her encouragement.

I had made one marvelous discovery during those

early days. I had a gift for making people laugh. I was the first-born son, and the only child for five years until Dan came along (Ken was born three years after that). I think my mother spoon-fed me herself until the moment he was born. But in school, my gift was not universally appreciated. I became a wise guy, a real smart ass, the class cutup. And there were many semesters when it landed me in my own special seat right in front of the teacher's desk.

By my teenage years, there was a war going on. The big "WWII" and the epic heroics grabbed my imagination. There was plenty to stimulate an adolescent boy's visions of bravery and romance.

Everyone had romantic notions about the war during that time. Newsreels, posters warning that "a slip of the lip will sink a ship," and that we would "remember Pearl Harbor" were commonplace. There were scrap drives, War Bond drives, and savings stamps we purchased at school each week, at twenty-five cents each. Meat, sugar, and gasoline were rationed, and I can remember hearing my mother worry and work at her red stamps. Shoes were very scarce, and since there were no nylons, patriotic women wore leg makeup. Lucky Strike Green went to war. The movies were all romantic, war-oriented films. We heard of the Bataan Death March; our radios were filled with the "Boogie Woogie Bugle Boy" and Bob Hope on tour around the world. There were soldiers and sailors everywhere. Every family that had a son, brother, sweetheart, or husband in the service had a service flag in the window—a small banner with a red border with a white field and, in the center, a blue star for each man in the service. If he were killed or missing or a POW, the star was gold. How we loved our servicemen. The USOs were so thick you could hit a

19

different one every night. Every girl worth her red stamps spent at least one night a week there. She would serve meals or coffee, or she would dance. She'd be happy to sew on a button or press a uniform or just talk.

I tried to enlist twice at age sixteen, and actually made it for twenty-four hours, winding up in an army induction center at Jefferson Barracks, outside St. Louis. But my parents found out and brought me home each time.

I wouldn't take "no" for an answer though, and by the next year, my seventeenth birthday, they acquiesced. My dad took me down to the naval recruiting office to sign the necessary papers because I was underage.

I did manage to wring the last ounce of dramatic impact from it all. We were doing a production of "Hit the Deck" at my high school, Cleveland High, and I was playing the chief petty officer. I came out in costume for our final dress rehearsal, and made my momentous announcement. Stunned silence, ohs, ahs—I savored all of it.

The navy was the formative experience for me and—I am sure—for many young men in that era. After boot camp at Great Lakes and radio school in Indianapolis, I became a radioman. Since I had tried to enlist twice before, I had taken the same Morse code test each time, but the navy had somehow never kept records. By the third time, I did so well I was labeled a natural for communications. I was attached to a communications security unit and trained to hit the beach at Okinawa.

Our mission was to copy Japanese code, to disrupt their communications, to track various ships and planes through RDF (Radio Direction Finding), and also to keep from getting killed—which is why they took away our hard-earned navy uniforms and made us look like marines. The marines weren't fooled; we were still swabbies to them. But they took care of us and most of us survived. Afterward, I was transferred to a security unit in Hawaii, where I stayed "frozen," as they say, until the first Eniwetok A-bomb tests were completed. I got out in 1946. By then the war had been over for a year and we servicemen were somewhat old hat, except to our families who were happy to finally have us home.

My brothers and I started to get close, I think, during World War II. I served but Dan and Ken were too young. When I came home it was a joy to see my brothers, and they were sure happy to see me.

College seemed anticlimactic by comparison. Being a sailor had already provided my initiation into adulthood. But I wanted to reenter the conventional world where school, education, and degrees were the keys to the kingdom. It was time to get on with life as quickly as possible. I picked up a high school equivalency diploma and enrolled at the University of Missouri. I could hardly believe how campuses were swollen with returning young, and not so young, GIs like myself. We were the norm during those postwar years, and college classes were huge. Professors were giving their lectures with megaphones. I didn't adjust well to that atmosphere. I had nothing in the way of study habits or discipline, and had not much prospect of learning, let alone coping with the chaos.

I was complaining to my dad one evening on the phone and again, he came to the rescue. He made arrangements for me to enroll at his old college, Hannibal-LaGrange, a small, mostly Baptist ministerial school also offering liberal arts, with about 1,500 students in Hannibal, Missouri—Mark Twain

Country on the banks of the Mississippi just north of St. Louis. I zipped through it all in three years, taking extra hours and summer sessions.

By the end of my junior year, I had rushed into something else—marriage. I met and married a nineteen-year-old coed named Helen Hill.

With degree in hand, I got a reporting job with the *Hannibal Courier-Post*, but I didn't get too comfortable in it. One of my responsibilities was to write the radio column once a week, and by the end of one month I heard that the radio station in Hannibal, KHMO—5000 watts day and night—needed a continuity writer. This is the individual who writes the commercials and reads them over the air. The job paid a whole five dollars more a week than the newspaper job, but I had to work gratis for one whole week to learn how to do it. The sacrifices I made for my craft! In those days we worried just about eating.

Helen was working at the station as well, as a traffic manager, meaning that she prepared the log (or schedule) for everything that went over the air. We had such illustrious advertisers as a local chicken feed manufacturer—remember I said this was America's heartland—and Lady Betty Silver. "Send one dollar, that's right, just one dollar for your three-piece place setting of Lady Betty Silver."

We also did commercials for "The Toy Man," "The Blade Man," and Hadacol tonic. I did a lot of live studio programming in addition to regular disc jockey work. How about "Sing Along with Cowboy Dallas Turner"? I had to get on the air with him to do his commercials, because although he could sing, he couldn't read. Then there was the biggie I did twice a day, "Ambrose Haley and the Ozark

Ramblers." And that's how I got my start in broadcasting!

But I was not destined to give up my dashing navy career so easily. Like a dummy I had stayed in the naval reserve, and I got a call from a chief petty officer friend of mine telling me I might get called back. Korea, a far-off, little-known country adjoining mainland China, was heating up, and terms like the 38th parallel and Panmunjom were becoming familiar, though exotic, to Americans.

Actually, when the recall to active duty came, I had only twenty-four hours, notice. My friend, the chief who had permanent duty at the naval reserve armory in town (a place I never visited), called to inform me that my orders were in, and that I would receive them by mail the following day. That was when I made my vain attempt to join the air force, only to learn that they had recently changed regulations and did not accept married men, even veterans.

So, I found myself back at Great Lakes facing two and one-half more years on active duty. I was assigned to a destroyer escort named the USS *Raby*. She was a rustbucket if there ever was one, and as a standard radioman I was virtually condemned, ball-and-chain style, to the ship's radio shack. However, battle stations had me on the bridge as port lookout.

My recollections are of long, terrible, terrible cruises—destroyers can be a rough ride—rotten weather, and an excitement quotient of zero.

The ship's home port was Norfolk, Virginia—Naw-Fawk to those of us with subtle intonations.

While I was serving Uncle Sam on the high seas, Helen stayed in Hannibal. At my pleading she came to Norfolk to visit and decided to stay. With the confidence of the young, she quit her job and packed up and moved across the country. Within two days, she walked into the local television station and got a job in the traffic department.

WTAR-TV was the only TV station in Norfolk. In those days, it had the service of NBC, CBS, ABC, and even the late lamented DuMont network. Still, there was a lot of local programming because there wasn't that much network service in the early fifties. Helen arranged for me to audition at the station a month before I was to get out of the navy.

I was hired on as a staff announcer. This meant sitting in an "announce booth" for an eight-hour shift, doing station breaks. This left me with a lot of time on my hands. So I made the most of it (again with the confidence and ignorance of the young), and within a year was writing, directing, and appearing on camera.

My first live shot was a job doing commercials for Canada Dry. I've often talked of that coincidence with Marilyn. While she did her first TV spots in London, Ontario, for Wishing Well Orange, a soda pop, I, in full costume as a soda jerk, was Canada Dry Charlie. They were carefully scripted commercials done live with a crowd of advertising agency executives watching. The advertisement appeared during "The Gene Autry Show." The cowboy and the jerk. Soda jerk. I was pathetic. My hands shook so badly that the ice cubes spun out of the glass and the pour missed the glass completely. Helen said that even in black and white, I was so pale she thought I was sick.

Later, having gained more confidence, I started doing spots for a local dairy. They had just acquired the now-common whipped cream in a pressurized can. On camera, live, we demonstrated topping a pie with whipped cream from the new pressurized can.

24

Unfortunately, the can was faulty and in no time the studio was filled with flying whipped cream, shooting forth as if the can were a fire hose. The stuff splattered me; the cream demonstrator screamed, dropped the can, and ran from the set before the director could regain his senses and fade to black. On another occasion, while doing a commercial for the same dairy, I was required to take a sip of milk, smile, look at the camera (which was in a tight close-up of my face), and quote the dairy's slogan. On the air, live, I sipped, choked, sprayed the lens with milk, and gasped, "Try Birtcherds and taste the difference." I was soon dropped by the dairy.

There were only fifty or sixty TV stations that were licensed and on the air before the federal government imposed a freeze on construction and licensing. When this was lifted, in about 1953, a virtual gold rush followed. In my infinite wisdom and vast two years' experience, one with radio in Hannibal, the other with TV in Norfolk, I decided it was time to move in the broadcasting world. I began reading the list of building and construction permits that was published in each issue of *Broadcasting Magazine, the* trade journal at that time.

I wrote to all of them. I wanted to get back to the Midwest, and the first person who answered was a guy in Rockford, Illinois, eighty-eight miles north and west of Chicago. I flew in for the interview and was hired as combination program director/production manager. These were pretty important responsibilities for one with such a limited track record. But then again, the guy who hired me was the station manager, who had just been a salesman before that.

But there were millions of opportunities to learn in those days—and I took them. Television was a new frontier. The rules and body of knowledge—

well, you filled it in as you went along. I remember one show with a lady who did crafts. Five minutes, once a day, *live*. One day while doing her shtick on the air, she shot her finger with a stapling gun, and it bled profusely. I was directing that one, and we wanted to do a close-up of what she was doing. I remember the camera zooming in for a close-up on the construction paper, with bright red fingerprints all over it slowly turning to brown. But she was a real trooper. She went through her five minutes with a smile firmly frozen on her face until the bitter end.

We stayed seven years in Rockford.

This was a real growth period in my life. As program director and general factotum, I was sort of the number-two man at the station. I learned a tremendous amount and thought I'd be making station management my lifelong career.

The town of Rockford, Illinois, a solid community near the Wisconsin border, has a heavy Swedish population. Helen's and my three children were born there in the Swedish-American Hospital. First came Kathleen, then a year later, John III, and finally, eighteen months after Johnny, came little Terri Lee.

While in Rockford, I learned how to fly airplanes, and the kids started to grow. None, however, were in school when we left this very nice town upon my accepting a job with WJIM-TV in Lansing, Michigan.

At WJIM-TV I was in production, but in those days of television, everyone did a little bit of everything. It was like summer stock. We needed an actor to play Ranger Jim for our local kids' show, so I became Ranger Jim.

We liked living in Lansing very much. We lived in suburban Okemos near a nine-hole golf course. The

26

station was in a beautiful building. The owner and general manager was a paradoxical creature. He could be a veritable Santa Claus, generous to a fault. But he would refuse to air-condition his TV studio, and only heavy pressure convinced him to repair a leak in the roof, and that was because it dripped on the anchorman's head when it rained. In spite of myself, I liked the tyrant, and he appeared to like me. But the battles wore me down, so when an offer came from Atlanta two years later, I jumped at it.

Atlanta, Georgia—it truly seemed like the big time to me. A big market, a big job, a big salary, and I was program director. Helen and I went with big plans. We packed up the three kids and purchased a big house accompanied by a very big mortgage. Shortly thereafter we went reeling, with a very big thud.

The station was sold within a year of my arrival, and after the new owners gave the standard reassurances to everyone that they were not going to make any radical changes, they began to systematically chop off the heads of each of the players in management. Mine was the last, so I got the chance to watch all of the other heads roll in the process.

I was strangely calm about it all. I turned the dining room into an office and began to write letters to every place I could think of. But in the back of my mind I started thinking that I had spent a lot of time in management, ten years by that point, and hadn't really had a chance to do what I wanted to do; to me that was beginning to mean broadcasting, and being in front of the camera lens.

I got a call from a fellow in Peoria, Illinois. He did something that is frequently done in this business, but seldom apparent if you are not on the inside. He thought I was still employed as program director, and wanted to know if there was anyone at the competing stations that I wanted to get out of town.

At that point, I certainly was in no position to get rid of any enemies. I told him the only person I wanted out of town was *me!*

He invited me to meet him in Chicago, and from there I went by train to Peoria for an audition. They were looking for an anchorman and, almost as an afterthought, the director asked me, in a disembodied voice from the control room, if I could ad-lib for the camera to demonstrate my eye contact. Words and ideas have always come to me when I've needed them, and they did at that moment. I gave a description of a cross-country train trip that I had taken a few years before, and it really sounded like a romantic travelogue. It was pure Rockwell in a word painting.

I was hired, and I was euphoric to have a job. The job was a big change for me. I went from behind the camera in an executive position to in front of it as talent. I was anchorman and reporter on the street and occasionally cameraman. It was great to be working again, although it was for thousands less than I had made in Atlanta.

I loved Peoria. For one thing, WMBD was the only station that offered to pay my moving expenses and provide me with a place to stay until I could sell the Atlanta house and move my family. For another, I was back in the Midwest, and that felt good. It was coming home. True, there was a new city to get used to, but it felt comfortable. I had had enough of the South. Atlanta was a beautiful city, but there was a pale beyond which Yankees did not go, at least at that time. My whole experience with the station there was a bitter one.

For six months I lived in a hotel at WMBD's

expense, while Helen and the children remained in Atlanta trying to sell our house. When the house sold, they packed up and joined me in Peoria.

We had done a lot of moving around by that time, but I don't think that I felt itinerant. Moving is inherent in broadcasting. You know that there are only so many jobs, at so many stations. For news anchors, as an example, there are only a certain number of plum jobs in big markets. If you want to get ahead, you have to be prepared to move to another city for another opportunity. But moving and starting over takes a toll on your family life. At least it did with mine, but in my professional fervor, I didn't see it.

When we moved to Peoria, Kathleen, the oldest of the children, was in first grade; Johnny, the second, was in kindergarten; and Terri Lee, the youngest, was in preschool.

Because money was short, Helen got a job. Surprisingly, it was at a competing station, which gave *my* bosses pause, but they soon accepted it.

Actually, it worked out fairly well. I worked nights, Helen worked days. The kids went off to school, all in the morning, and she went off to work. I'd be up midmorning to pick up the kids for lunch at home, which always was fun for me. On a nice day we'd have cheeseburgers and french fries and cokes for a little picnic in a nearby park. I would leave as our high-school-age sitter arrived for a couple of hours, then Helen was home to take charge. The next year Terri was spending a full day in school. I still had lunch with them, and a sitter was waiting when they all got home.

As I think back, they were wonderful kids. The problem was that Helen and I never saw each other aside from the weekend, and only one day of that because I was working six nights a week, early and late news.

The opportunity in Detroit came innocuously enough. For about two years, I had been grinding out the news six nights a week in Peoria. A representative from Storer Broadcasting Company called me one day and said that they had taped my work and liked the way I looked and sounded. Would I be interested in working for their operation?

I told them I would—anywhere but in Atlanta, because I knew that Storer had a station there. The fellow said they were interested in me for the flagship station—Detroit. Could I come and have a look at things?

My first meeting with anyone from Detroit was with news director Bob McBride. It was May 1965. I had yet to be hired; it depended on his impression of me, and viceversa. Strangely, I really was not that excited.

At the time, my brother Dan was living in Chelsea, Michigan, serving a church there. We took a week's vacation, loaded up the kids, and took off for Chelsea. Then I proceeded to Detroit for the interview.

I had never been in Detroit. I hadn't been on a freeway in over two years. WJBK at the time was located in the new Center area, at Second and Bethune, just across from what used to be Saks Fifth Avenue. Channel 56, the PBS station, is in the old WJBK building now. Following precise directions, I found the place and spent about two hours with Bob McBride. The newsroom was small but to me it looked big. Later we had lunch, then spent a couple of hours driving around the city and suburbs in Bob's Mustang convertible. He pointed out places of interest and told me of the news situation in the city.

We parted on a very friendly note with his promise of calling me to let me know if I was hired. By then I wanted the job!

Later we drove from Chelsea to Chicago, where my parents were living at the time following a transfer Dad had received. From their house, I called McBride to tell him I was definitely interested. He told me that I had the job.

They offered me two conditions that looked very attractive: a five-night-a-week job instead of the six that I was doing in Peoria, and a lot more money.

So there we were: Helen thinking about moving—again! The kids thinking about settling into new schools and neighborhoods—again! They had started to realize what "public celebrity" meant in Peoria, and they were not entirely thrilled with the prospect. Me, I was thinking about a new market, a big market, again! Kelly was looking pretty good—moving out—moving on—and moving up.

3
FAIR SKIES, STEADILY RISING TEMPERATURES

MARILYN

Right from the start, February 5, 1931, I was one of those children who is "special." Mother was an only child, and my father only had one brother. I was the first grandchild on both sides, the first granddaughter in generations. And secretly, inside my head, I have always harbored the belief that I was born ahead of my time. If I had been born later, things might have been a little easier for me. At least there might have been some role models to follow. The decisions that I made in the late fifties and early sixties—namely, to pursue a career, to raise children, to avoid the stereotyped image of the successful doctor's wife who pursues the endless bridge game— were certainly unusual for the times, though they seemed to me the most natural and honest way to go on with my life.

Consciously, I never set out with a master plan. I never thought about where I would be in five years, or ten, or what kind of strategies I would use to get there. But unconsciously, I believe I must have *really* wanted that career. It was not easy. I had to break the ice, each step of the way. What is more, I have had to define my own rules and have had to fight for a lot of things along the way. I still do—in this business I don't think that ever stops. In fact, there is an axiom in show business: the bigger you are, the more you have to look out for yourself.

From my earliest memories, I was always performing. I can't ever remember an instance of having stage fright. When I was no more than two or three, my parents would take me to present dramatic readings at local town hall meetings, Kiwanis clubs, or parent-teacher get-togethers in neighboring towns. Those were my first acting experiences. As soon as I was old enough for the teachers to accept me, Mother enrolled me in tap, ballet, voice, acrobatics, the whole gamut of lessons. By age four I was a genuine advertising celebrity—Miss Hydro, a Canadian government-sponsored campaign—with my picture on billboards around southern Ontario!

It was an intense life for someone so young. I was heavily programmed, but I innately understood the benefits that come with being attractive and pleasing. I innately understood that I had something "special" as well.

I've always had a certain independent streak, too, right from the very beginning. There were many times when I rebelled. In fact, the Miss Hydro contest, a great success for someone so young, led to an episode that brought about a temporary standstill in my budding career.

My mother had taken me to a photographer for

some portraits in connection with that contest. The photographer lived a few blocks away and Mother dropped me off, with plans to pick me up in an hour. At age four, I got restless and bored posing. The photographer had gone off in a back room someplace and was wasting a lot of time. I decided that I didn't want to be there at all. I picked up and walked out—and home! All by myself. Mother considers that a momentous event—my first outburst of temperament—and my performing career was put on hold.

I have felt that way since—not often, but at certain critical turning points, I have picked myself up and walked away. The two most important instances that occur to me were my marriage and my work. My first husband, Bob Turner, never wanted our divorce, neither the first nor the second time after we remarried six years later. But I simply couldn't and wouldn't put up with certain things, and luckily my career had taken hold so that I didn't have to.

Then there was the issue of my early television work, the national commercials that I was doing in New York City and Chicago. It was wonderful work, exciting and extremely lucrative. But I reached a point where it just wasn't worth it any more. I wasn't getting anywhere.

I had been flying to New York or Chicago, usually for a couple of weeks at a time, probably about five times a year, to audition for national commercials. This went on for six or seven years, and I hit successfully on some big ones. Suddenly, I hit a dry spell—nothing seemed to be coming together.

On one of these trips, I auditioned for thirteen jobs, which took about two weeks. I didn't get a callback from any of them. I was disappointed and depressed. I decided to go home. I called my agent from LaGuardia and announced that I was not going to come back for any more auditions. He told me not to be silly, that I had just hit a dry spell and it happened to everyone in the business.

I never did go back. At last, the pain had exceeded the pleasure, a motto that I apply to many things in my life.

That was a decisive move that affected my way of life. There are certain traits in my character that I've come to recognize. Decisiveness is one of them. I've got a pretty good temper, I admit it, and at times it has helped me. And I also know that I am good in front of a camera. My mother recognized that and did everything she could to help me develop any talent that I had.

My mother was a dedicated movie fan, and my maiden name was Marilyn Miller, just like the musical comedy star who was popular in the twenties and thirties. I don't think my mother chose the name deliberately, but she was quick to make comparisons and sense the possibilities in me. As soon as it was possible to curl my hair into corkscrews, I had them, just like Shirley Temple.

Marilyn Monroe used to be a Marilyn Miller too— when she was married to Arthur Miller. With that coincidence in mind, I have become a tremendous Marilyn Monroe fan over the years. I have photos of her all over my house.

My extended family was small and we all basically lived in Windsor, Ontario. I was born in Windsor and spent a great deal of my early life there. My father was a manager for the Canadian oil company, Supertest. We were transferred about 125 miles away to London, Ontario, for four years and then another year in Barrie, a small town north of Toronto.

As an only child, I never wished for brothers or

sisters. I was always very involved in activities and always had lots of friends. But, paradoxically, I sometimes found myself wishing there were a sister or brother around to take some of the heat so my parents would get off my back. Looking back, it's easy to see why my parents' worries and concerns, their hopes and expectations, became a burden at times, and it's equally easy to understand *them*. However, at the time, I became a bit of a rebel.

When we moved to London, my rebellion continued. I refused to do a lot of the lessons that I had been programmed into—I wanted to play. I got involved in figure skating, joined a figure skating club, and gave up everything else for the four years or so that we lived there.

One summer there was a polio epidemic in London. In those days, polio was a fearsome disease, and it was leaving young children paralyzed for life. So my parents packed me up and sent me back to Windsor to live with my grandparents for the summer.

Then we moved again, just for one year, up north to Barrie for my father's job. I have always been more energetic than contemplative, but I remember being more aware of nature—the flowers and the trees, huge pine trees—than ever before. I was nine years old during the year we lived in Barrie, and I remember it with great fondness. I embraced the winter sports—skiing, tobogganing, and, of course, skating on the lake at our doorstep. It was a different life than what I had known before, but a pleasant and picturesque one, and I fell in love with the uniqueness of it.

I remember making friends with a family who lived in a tent all year round. They lived near a small, pondlike lake that I passed each morning as I walked to school. They weren't Indians; they just lived in a tent, and it could get very cold in northern Ontario. I thought they were neat, and I befriended them. I also remember that my mother did not approve—but that didn't stop me.

When we moved back to Windsor, I became involved in everything again—school plays, cheerleading, and even twice-a-week accordion lessons. That was important for a couple of reasons. First, I soon began playing all over Windsor at banquets, weddings, and PTA meetings. I liked it. I was in my early teens, and I began noticing boys. And that's the second reason the accordion was important: I met my first boyfriend. He was just twelve years old, and was also on the program at a PTA meeting. His name was Bill Fellows, he was a soprano, and he had blonde, curly hair. I was smitten!

SYLVIA STRAITH

Marilyn and I go back a long way. We were high school chums. We dated some of the same boys, even double-dated occasionally. Marilyn has always been used to male attention; that's a basic fact of life for her. She enjoys flirting, whether she's in a group or not. It's an inborn thing with her; she creates an aura of "Yes, I'm a woman, and you're a man." This may sound silly now, but it's the truth. Marilyn was the high school glamour girl. But that wasn't threatening to me because she was so down to earth. Basically, she hasn't changed. She may wear different hats because of different roles, but she's still the same, and it's one of the reasons I like her. I think most people would be surprised at how absolutely, completely down to earth Marilyn is. I watched her when she made her own clothes when she was modeling and when she did the weather at Channel Two. Once I went on an audition with her—oh, years ago—and here we are, all dressed to the nines, driving a secondhand car and laughing all the way because we're looking at the road through holes in the floor of the car. She's paid her dues; she's earned every cent. She has great self-discipline. For instance, she loves food, but she absolutely will not allow herself to put on weight. She's been that way ever since I've known her. Yeah, self-discipline is Marilyn's biggest strength; she has complete security in herself and manages to wring every little bit out of life.

MARILYN

I was still involved in skating, both in competition and freestyle. When I was about sixteen or seventeen, the Ice Capades were making an appearance in Windsor. They typically hold tryouts in many of the cities they visit. I heard about the upcoming tryouts through the network of skating friendships I had, and I went down to the audition with a friend. There must have been about twenty people evaluating us, and we both made it. I really wanted to do it and my girlfriend actually did go, but my parents were planning on my going to college, and they did not want me doing anything of the sort.

I was upset for a while. I don't know exactly what my motivations were. Maybe I was looking for an opportunity to break away and leave home. The big traveling shows like the circus or the Ice Capades usually sign on young women for the chorus for about two years at a stretch, so it would certainly have delayed my entrance to college, and maybe jeopardized my going at all. Thank goodness for

Mom and Dad. It really would have been a rough life—awful unless I had been a headliner.

At the time, however, it seemed as though years and years of skating were going down the drain. Later, when my own two sons both skated in Little League hockey teams during their school years, I spent many, many more hours in ice rinks, cheering them on. Dean, the younger of the two, actually did confront me with the dilemma of leaving college to play hockey professionally. I let him go, which meant that he was leaving college after his freshman year. I made this decision, but not with any sense of absolute conviction that it was the right thing to do. I lived to see myself in the same position my parents were in twenty-five years earlier.

So I stayed in high school, stayed in Windsor, performed with my accordion, had boyfriends and dates, and was involved in dozens of other activities. Upon graduation, I followed the path that my parents had planned for me. I enrolled in the University of Western Ontario, in London.

I met Bob Turner at the registration tables on the first day of my first semester at the University of Western Ontario. It was a warm, beautiful early fall day in September 1950, and the whole scene was almost too good to be true. It could have come straight out of a movie script: Betty Co-ed goes to college and meets the campus hero her first day out. He was tall, six feet two, physically rugged, and handsome, strikingly handsome. There was some Indian ancestry way back on his mother's side (they were from Lethbridge, Alberta), and there was a suggestion of that in his high, wide cheekbones.

Aside from his physical appearance, Bob Turner was charming and sexy, and considered quite a "catch." He was a varsity football player and a good student who was planning to go to med school.

I know now I had a mental picture of that "Mr. Right," but in this case it was *any* Mr. Right. *He* had to fit *my* image! Blonde, medical student, and if he was an athlete, so much the better. Sort of a bonus, I suppose. As it happened, I went with Bill Fellows through high school, knowing he was going to medical school, and he still had those blonde curls. During the summer between high school and college, I met another pre-med student. You guessed it—blonde, too! But in the fall came those registration tables and Bob Turner. Blonde, pre-med, and an athlete. It would have been impossible to anticipate any of the difficulties that were to haunt Bob Turner later. But I suppose the clues are there if you look for them.

For one thing, his family had gone from riches to rags, not an easy direction to travel in. His father, Alfred F. Turner, had been a physician, a general practitioner in Kitchener, Ontario, and the family had been well-off. Bob was the oldest of four kids. There was Frank, who was just one year younger; a sister, Eileen, who was exactly my age; and a sister, Yvonne. Bob was just sixteen when his father died, suddenly and prematurely, of a heart attack at the age of fifty-three. For some reason, he had canceled his insurance policies shortly before he died, and the family was hit hard financially. Bob's mother, whom everyone nicknamed "Whitey" after her maiden name of Whiteside, was a reserved, dignified woman who had always had steady household help and led a life of ease and leisure. To me, she always seemed much older than her years. She moved slowly, and was certainly much different from my own mother who was quick and agile. Bob told me later that the maids who worked for the family would take charge of getting the kids off to school—that it was his mother's custom to sleep until ten in the morning, no matter what.

Mrs. Turner was definitely not prepared for widowhood. Before her husband's death, she had never handled finances, or even used a checkbook, and here she was with four children to educate.

It was a common practice forty years ago for physicians to set up their offices in their homes, and that was the case with Bob's father. Virtually penniless, Whitey was forced to sell her husband's medical practice. Sadly, the doctor who bought the practice also bought the house, which he used as medical offices. The Turner family was forced to live in what had been their maids' quarters. Whitey did housecleaning for the new family and returned to practicing nursing, which she had done early in her marriage. Years later, when things got stormy in my marriage, I forgave Bob a lot of things, knowing what rough times he had experienced.

He didn't ask me out for three months; December 9th was our first date. In the meantime, that fall I was getting into sports. I dated two or three football players and had great fun! But I was convinced that Bob was the man for me. We got engaged that April, and we were married the following August. Marriage was in the air, I guess. Just one month before, we had attended Bob's sister Eileen's wedding, and Bob, acting his father's role, gave the bride away.

My parents were very much opposed. I had only had one year of college, and with Bob about to start medical school, they felt we were rushing into things. This time I overruled. I wanted to get married. I could not see the practicalities or the impracticalities of our plans, and they couldn't convince me of anything else. Looking back, I must have been absolutely insane! At the time I was *insanely* in love, and it *did* last thirteen years, through a lot of ups and downs that neither of us could have foreseen.

Our wedding was small, not lavish—my parents could not have afforded that—but pretty and romantic, with all of the classic trimmings. I had a short white gown and veil, a bridal party, a church ceremony, and an afternoon reception in my parents' yard. The date was August 25th, one week before medical school classes were scheduled to start, and the anniversary of Bob's father's birthday.

If I thought I'd covered a lot of ground in my first year of college, that pattern certainly didn't change much the year after that. By the following year, I was not only married but a mother besides. Our first son, Robert Ross Turner, was born August 28th. We were prepared to struggle through. We knew it would be tight for us financially, but there were other couples in similar circumstances. We figured that we could live on very little. In fact, we felt that if we made $125 a month, we could stay afloat.

But having a child certainly changed things. My parents had offered to pay our first year's rent as a wedding present, and to be thrifty, we had rented a modest apartment in London, located over a funeral home overlooking a Chinese laundry.

At least, that was the plan, and it didn't call for having children. In the early fifties you didn't see pregnant women engaging in nondomestic activities very much. The prevailing attitude was that if you were pregnant, you stayed home. That attitude never stopped me from accomplishing my goals and going on with my activities, whatever they happened to be at the moment. At that moment, I wanted to complete my degree at Teacher's College, near the University. But the attitudes of the times did create a certain amount of inner turmoil. I can recall feeling self-conscious and actually embarrassed about being pregnant during that first pregnancy. There weren't any other women "in the family way" at Teachers' College that year. At least there weren't any who were married and in the circumstances to let their condition be public. Yet here I was, wearing maternity clothes, generally with white collars and little bows at the neckline. I had always thought of myself as a compact and active person, and now I was literally filling an entire seat on the bus that I'd take to classes.

Television had come a bit later to Canada than to the United States and it lagged behind in live programming and availability of talent for quite awhile. The station in London had been built in the early fifties; most of its hours on the air were filled with old movies. Commercials, what there were of them, were mostly voiceovers with a static photograph that would come on the screen for thirty seconds.

I finally managed to get my degree and we moved down the street from the apartment over the funeral home to a duplex with a small yard. It was apparent that we needed money and both of us had to be resourceful to bring in whatever we could.

Two nights a week I was teaching an exercise class for a woman who ran a local modeling school. Then there was substitute teaching, which paid a grand total of $15 a day, out of which had to come money for a baby-sitter for Rob.

One day Bob came home and said he had read on the bulletin board at medical school about an audition that was being held for a girl to do a soft drink advertisement. I decided to try my luck—with about 100 other applicants. Miraculously, I won.

The job at the TV station consisted of doing a commercial every Sunday afternoon for Wishing Well Orange, a locally bottled soft drink, saying a few lines, and pouring the drink in front of the camera. The commercials were wrapped around old westerns, John Wayne or Hopalong Cassidy, and I was paid a grand total of $12.50 a show.

At first I'm sure I was awful. I had to learn how to look at the camera and pour from the bottle at the same time. That took a few trials and all of my athletic coordination, but I mastered that. Then one night I forgot my lines, right on the air. We planned to leave for a visit to my family right after the show, and I remember crying all the way between London and Windsor. I was sure I was going to be fired. But as I said, TV was quite new to Canada at that time, and the standards were not that exacting. No one at the station thought it serious enough to fire me. Quickly, Bob and I saw that it made more sense for me to work for an hour or two on Sunday afternoons at the TV station for $12.50 than to put in a whole day of teaching for $15.00, which required paying a baby-sitter besides.

In those early days, Bob was encouraging and supportive of my work. We needed the money, and he was proud of the fact that I could earn it. Unfortunately, in subsequent years, he felt that he had created a monster by encouraging me the way he did. But not then. It was fine in his eyes to work because you had to, but to choose a career as a way of life—well, it shouldn't get in the way of *his* career!

I had no master plan in those days. We were simply being as enterprising as we could to get along. Despite our modest circumstances and our day-to-day struggles, there were many fun times. Our friends were all in similar circumstances, and all of them were doing the best they could to scrape along financially. Bob's younger brother, Frank, was married, in medical school, and had three small children. We spent time with them, and his wife and I often pooled baby-sitting detail.

The Sunday afternoon television commercial was no "star trip." No one thought it was exceptional or out of the ordinary. But even then, when I was pretty naive about the business of performing, I began to realize how much those years of doing commercials in London, Ontario, were worth in terms of experience. It is critically important to get that kind of on-the-air exposure in a small market before you can tackle a bigger one. When young people ask me how to break into this business, I always say, "Don't start with Detroit. Start in a small market where the pressures are not as great. First, try places like Traverse City, then inch your way into bigger markets." London, and those years of pouring Wishing Well Orange in front of the camera during the Sunday afternoon western, was that small, relatively pressure-free market for me.

Medical school stretched from 1952 through 1955, and *we* stretched every dollar we made; and in truth it was more like pennies. Bob worked at LaBatts Brewery in the summers (as did many students), and I picked up every television job I could find, commercials and, for a while, a five-minute daily exercise show. I started a class in modeling and self-improvement. It wasn't easy, but we had a goal: get him through medical school! By 1954–55 Bob was finishing medical school and considering specializing. All I would think of (and I said it to Bob) was: will it ever end? Another four years? He chose psychiatry and entered a four-year residency at the Ontario

46

Hospital in London. An unfortunate choice. After six months of spending night and day with more than just *very* disturbed patients (some had been in the back wards for thirty years!), he was ready to become a patient himself. Bob changed specialties and chose the "happier" field, obstetrics. He also lost a whole year because his psychiatric residency was of no use in acquiring accreditation for OB/GYN.

In Canada you almost had to pay the hospital for four years just to get in at that time. I know the pay is low now, no matter what country, but in the late fifties it was literally nothing! With four years ahead and with a child, a resident had to be subsidized, which we were not. Checking into the U.S., Bob found that we could at least make a living wage. As a matter of fact, depending on location, there was a wide range of benefits. We chose Oakwood Hospital in Dearborn because the salary was passable and they were offering *free* housing. Can you imagine what that sounded like after five long years of struggling? Heaven sent! And there was more! It was not just "housing," but an honest-to-goodness *house*. It was small, but I thought it was magnificent, and I had my very first washer and dryer. We were definitely "moving on up."

Like some sort of modern-day Goldilocks, I tried this new-found state of luxury for exactly one month. I was restless and decided to check out the local television stations.

It was to become a pattern; whenever I found myself with time on my hands, I went out and got a job. I know now that I am fiercely independent. I don't like to have to *ask* anyone for permission to do anything. For Bob and me, that particular trait manifested itself in the issue of money. I simply can't imagine myself going to a man and asking for it, ever.

I was so naive, I decided to take on the challenge of Detroit's three television stations on a Saturday afternoon in the summer of 1957. Fortunately, however, I have learned a few things about doing business in this business since.

Of course no one was around, except for one ad salesman at Channel Four. Ron Gilbert was his name. I'll never forget him. He told me that he had heard that Channel Two was looking for a young woman to do the weather. That accidental meeting charged my life.

Channel Two's weather spot was jokingly called the Fertile Weather Board in those days. They were always looking for someone to do the weather! None of the women they hired ever seemed to last more than six months before they would become pregnant and take maternity leave.

My tender experience in London, in Canadian television, had served me well. I was hired for the weekend weather.

In no time at all, I fell right into the rhythm of the job. A few months later I became pregnant.

Dean Cameron Turner was born June 22, 1958, just as Bob was finishing his first year of residency at Oakwood Hospital. I *did* take off three months, all told, but the weather job, being on Saturdays and Sundays, did not take too much time away from the family.

We purchased a small home in Dearborn, near Oakwood Hospital, where upon finishing his residency, Bob went into practice with a Dr. Melvin Dennis who had delivered Dean.

I signed up with several local modeling agencies and became very "hot," as they say in the business, doing photo and film work, nearly all of it involving cars. Detroit was the car capital of the world after all. Generally, I was posed as a housewife and mother; in cars, next to cars, carrying groceries to and from cars—I was kept very busy. Soon I was able to hire live-in help full-time. With Bob at long last making some fairly good money and my various jobs, we were climbing the financial ladder. But when I look back now, I know that as we climbed, we lost each other.

With live-in help, I found that juggling work and children was not particularly difficult at all. And I made another discovery—that I was not interested in the wives' groups, country club outings, or card games that other physicians' wives were getting involved with to fill their days. I had developed a close and important friendship with a neighbor, Marg Lee, whose husband was also a physician on Oakwood's staff and who lived around the block from me, but I definitely didn't fit the syndrome of the good "doctor's wife." That fierce, terrible, little streak of independence asserted itself again. I recognized that I enjoyed having my own circle of friends, and that I loved the happy-go-lucky, loose camaraderie down at the television station on Second Boulevard on Saturday and Sunday nights.

A few years later, while I was visiting my parents in Windsor, a former neighbor, a young man who had been a friend from childhood, stopped by to say hello. He had just moved to New York and was working as a model. He told me that I really ought to do the same thing, that I was enormously photogenic, and that he thought I would have no difficulty getting commercial and endorsement jobs.

No one had presented me with those observations quite that directly before. I had already started doing commercials for some local companies, Star Furniture, Chatham Foods, and Carpet Center, as a spokesperson, but I had not thought of the possibilities of performing in commercials for television in national markets such as New York or Chicago. Besides, I had a family. I couldn't see myself going off to New York. "You don't have to," my friend assured me. "You can do it from here. Fly in for the interviews and audition for the parts you want. . . ."

This man was doing extremely well—I had seen his picture in many popular magazines. All those years of performing, all of those lessons, all of those competitions in skating and in childhood beauty contests came to the forefront and galvanized my energy. If he could go off to New York and start a successful modeling career, why couldn't I?

EILEEN TURNER

Bobby introduced me to Marilyn just when they were about to become engaged. Marilyn and I were both nineteen at the time, and I, too, was planning on getting married that summer. She was just gorgeous when I met her and not hard to get to know. We took a liking to one another immediately. If anything, she may have been a bit more introverted than she is now.

Even though she was naturally pretty, she knew how to accentuate her looks. She spent a great deal of time on herself. I wasn't used to someone who primped so much, and I was absolutely fascinated by her. Sometimes, I'd compliment her on her hair or her makeup, but Marilyn was never smug. Just the opposite. She'd usually reply: "Well, Eileen, I have to look good, because that's my job."

Marilyn had enormous self-confidence. I think this must have developed because her parents had encouraged her to take lessons and try so many things at an early age, and she was good at all of them. In those early days, I'm sure that trait attracted my brother to her. Later, when this sense of confidence turned into ambition, I think his admiration became more complicated and even ambivalent. But the issues were simpler when they were just starting out in married life, and I know he enjoyed the money that she started making.

But there is the other side to all of it. I think each found it very hard to be supportive of the other, and they ultimately rubbed each other raw as the pressures of two careers built and intensified.

Maybe their characters just wouldn't allow it. They were very competitive. I remember shortly after the summer of our weddings, mine in July and Marilyn and Bob's in August, we had some family portraits taken by a local photographer. The proofs came back and the whole family was together in my mother's living room looking them over. Marilyn and Bob were both fiercely interested in their own photos and how they each looked, and I was struck by how little concern they showed for one another's.

Bob was a passionate person, and passionate in the way he expressed himself. I think he tried very hard in his short lifetime to be happy, and he certainly had romantic and idealistic notions about happiness. He had lots of friends and was basically a good guy. But there was something elusive and complex about him. As he started to gain success and stature in his obstetrics practice in Dearborn, and Marilyn became more involved with television, she'd want to talk about TV and he'd interrupt to talk about medicine. She quite obviously had achieved some prominence of her own. Not only was she doing the weather, but she did commercials on a regular basis for some local companies.

There seemed to be so many things in conflict. He wanted to be top dog, and with Marilyn no one can really be that. With her, any relationship has to be on an equal footing.

Unfortunately, the relationship took on even more sinister overtones. Bob became jealous of Marilyn around the time that she started traveling to New York and Chicago for auditions in the early sixties. Generally she would go for a week, maybe two weeks at a time, coming back to do the weekend weather.

I think that Bob probably had his reasons for feeling jealous. To begin with, it certainly wasn't common twenty years ago for a woman to be traveling for her career. I think he became very jealous of that streak of independence that Marilyn has. If only she could have needed *him* more.

4
HAS ANYBODY HERE SEEN KELLY?

JOHN

A month later we were in Detroit. My immediate boss was Carl Cederberg. Carl had been in the city a long time and knew everyone there was to know. His title was assignment editor, but in reality he was that as well as producer and assistant news director. Both he and Bob McBride took an immediate interest in every newscast. In those days, they were only thirty minutes long, including sports, weather, and commercials! I was in hog heaven when I learned that we had a cameraman and a sound man on every story—with a reporter it was a three-man crew. There were no women then, either as reporters, camera operators, or in sound. They did weather or were secretaries. 1965 was different all right.

It was all film in news. Videotape was two inches wide and on huge reels in tape machines that were bigger than most folks' refrigerators. Film was processed by our own staff in our own film lab. It was good quality too.

The promised five-day week at Channel Two lasted only about six months. I was quickly back to working on Saturdays thereafter. But Detroit was the fifth largest television market at that time, and they had made a spot for me, complete with a big promo campaign. "Has Anybody Here Seen Kelly?" was how it went. Everyone was looking for me because I was out on the street, hustling up stories. At least, that was the logic behind this ten-second hard-sell.

The salary increase was "for real," too. I got $17,000 as a street reporter and six o'clock anchor, which was enough to be able to put my financial life in order after the devastation of Atlanta. I would be out on the streets until about three in the afternoon and then the news director would pull me into the station to prepare for the evening news show at six.

Juggling the two roles seemed to be no big deal—there were only about fifteen minutes of news that we were responsible for—at least in the beginning. And local newsmen were all still attempting to sound like John Cameron Swayze. But that was destined to change. Local news had not yet become major business to television, but it was poised for a takeoff.

What made that so? What contributed? I'd say that the nature of the events of the times had a great deal to do with it, starting in the sixties with the Kennedy assassination and on through the seventies. Then there were competitive pressures from management who thought first and foremost about the business of television, and finally, the expanding electronic capability of the medium itself.

I think we sensed this growing importance of local news coverage, and we were all eager beavers—

aggressive and fired up with the idea that we could build a good news department for Channel Two.

Most of us were willing and ready to work our heads off for the sheer excitement of it all. Jerry Cavanaugh was Detroit's mayor at the time, and the city was bustling with a kind of vitality that was infectious.

As a street reporter you quickly learn your way around in a big city. After all, you have a mission to accomplish each night at six. I befriended some of the behind-the-scenes types. A cameraman named Murray Young was very helpful to me in those first few months. We'd spend hours together driving around Detroit while he rattled off street names and bits of local history.

I not only learned to move around like a native but also to sound like one. For example, it is *Char*lotte, in North Carolina; but Char*lotte*, in Michigan. I got used to the fact that the river ran from east to west, instead of the river I remember from my childhood in St. Louis—the Mississippi—which runs north and south.

I learned Detroit and its nooks and crannies. There was the glittering facade, and Detroit certainly had that in the sixties, but it also had the darker crevices. I got to know people—many different kinds of people—from many avenues. I developed a network of snitches on the street. *Snitch* is a word borrowed from the police. *Informant* or *tipster* would be more accurate. They were from all walks of life: street people, drug addicts, pimps, good solid citizens, anyone who was in a spot where he or she was privy to rumors and was willing to pass them along— mostly people who liked to talk and who, of course, could not be identified as a source.

For the working press, there were the privileges

and perks—like having the mayor give you a signal before a press conference because he has something important to tell you, or having the police chief recognize you and call you by name. It was exciting.

We felt like the infantry, the cavalry, and the light brigade—all rolled into one. We carried the camera in our cars and beepers hanging at our waists.

What was even more important—the station put its faith and trust in me to a degree that went beyond its advertising promo campaign. By 1966, Jac Le Goff and I were teamed up as anchors together at six and eleven. Jac was considered the old pro at Two, even then, and he had been doing the eleven o'clock news alone. Channel Four, headed by anchors Ven Marshall and Dick Westercamp, had been the powerhouse in Detroit, but as a team, Jac and I soon knocked them off. We stayed on top for years after that, and were, in fact, still on top when I left for WXYZ seven years later.

But, in time, my own role quickly grew much larger than anchoring. I had evolved into a kind of unofficial editor without portfolio. When I came in off the street at three o'clock, I'd go into a conference with the news director, Bob McBride, and the assignment editor, Carl Cederberg, where we would hash out the budget and the expectations for the day. We would assemble the six o'clock show—I'd write it, work with reporters, edit it, even figure out visuals and graphics that were really far beyond our electronic capabilities at the time. But I had been a director. My days in Rockford with wounded crafts ladies had left their mark, and the director and I understood each other. He was willing to try things, and the station was willing to spend the bucks. Local television news was just starting to flex its muscles.

If I wanted a helicopter to cover a story, I got a

helicopter. I had the authority to call people in. I remember the Port Huron Tunnel disaster in December 1971. The tunnel collapsed, and twenty-seven people were trapped inside and died. I first started to send a crew out in that direction, but when they phoned in to say how bad it was, I decided that we needed a reporter.

By then it was very late into the evening, getting close to air time. Vic Caputo, a wonderful guy who is now working as anchorman in Tucson, lived on the East Side and was a street reporter at that time. I called Vic out of an Italian-American dinner, tuxedo and all, and sent a single engine plane out to take him to the scene. There he was standing in a foot of muddy water with his tuxedo rolled up to his knees, but on camera, getting the story.

THE STANDOUTS

The standout stories are easy to remember. In the summer of 1967 we covered the largest, deadliest, most costly race riot. First, the National Guard was called in, then the regular army began patrolling the streets of Detroit in tanks, armored cars, and armored personnel carriers. Everything from .38 caliber revolvers to .50 caliber machine guns mounted on weapons-carriers with tracers could be heard slashing through the night. I'll never forget it. At times, on the streets of Detroit, it was war. I worked from 6:00 P.M. through the night to 6:00 A.M. My partner, Jac Le Goff, took the other twelve hours. Reporters and camera crews from all over the world used our station as a base, including John Hart and John Lawrence of CBS news as well as media people from England, Japan, West Germany, and the Netherlands.

I stood on the roof of WJBK and watched people smash windows and loot Saks Fifth Avenue and an S&H green stamp redemption center. On one occasion, bullets penetrated our building. Jack McCarthy, now a Channel Seven food critic and restauranteur, was the first Detroit newsman involved in the riots on the day it began on Twelfth Street. The newscar was stoned, and Jack was slugged before they got behind police lines and got out. That week in the summer of 1967, Detroit gained a reputation that never entirely left us.

Then, in 1968, there was the wonderful World Series win, and ball players that I knew were champions. The Detroit that urged, "Sock it to 'em, Tigers" was a very different city from the one of the previous summer.

You could always hunt up stories at 1300 Beaubien, Central Police Headquarters, a world unto itself. The police were guarded, but sometimes they would talk to reporters. Sometimes you could catch the bad guys in court.

One time one of the old-line bad guys, believed to be Mafia—I will not name him—was in Wayne County Circuit Court. We were set up in the hall, as were all the other reporters, waiting to grab him or his lawyer when they left the courtroom. I think the trial was murder or accessory, I'm not sure. But in the underworld, he was important. A silk suit type. I had my microphone close by and as the wait went on with games of "Hit and Spread," a sort of reporter's gin rummy, going on atop camera cases, we waited. One of the boys, after about an hour said, "He's coming out." Murray Young, my cameraman, said I should grab the mike and get up to the door. Of course, he didn't care; he was a safe twenty feet away. I was eager and so I did it. The lights were on.

Cameras were rolling and everyone was shouting, but I got there first. To this day I don't know what I said, but I *do* know he swung a foot at my genitals. Displaying athletic agility I didn't know I had, I leaped backward at least ten feet. He missed, but also I missed getting an answer. Or maybe the kick was it!

Another time, I got a woman junkie. She wasn't a snitch. She was just a pathetic heroin addict. She had an enormous habit and was too old to be a hooker, so she was a petty thief. All her veins had collapsed, and she was reduced to taking the needle under her tongue. She talked about it on camera because she wanted money for junk. I couldn't bring myself to give it to her, and she cursed us all the way out. I can still hear that voice. But we used the film.

We were always looking for the scoop. It had been learned that the owner-operator of a suburban cemetery had been misleading clients—the live ones. Among other things, he sold the most choice and therefore most expensive lots for burial over and over again—the same lots. He would hold the services, and when the grieving families departed, he'd exhume the coffin and do the whole thing over again. In the meantime, he stored remains in cemetery buildings until deciding what to do with them. He was also charged with selling expensive markers, purported to be several inches thick and of fine marble. The real markers, which were flat on the ground at the grave site, were thin and cheap. All of this alleged activity was illegal, and he went to trial. During this time, we got a hot tip that a woman was at the cemetery with a court order to open her mother's grave. Loading up, we tore out there and found the woman. With mike dangling at my side and cameras as discreet as a camera could be, I

59

callously explored the woman's agony. "Where," she cried to me and her friend, "is my mother?" It was the stuff that Emmy awards are made of. As she finished, I saw a Channel Seven truck in the distance; I immediately told her to go home, and we fled to our vehicle. As we were leaving, I waved smugly at Channel Seven reporter Bob Maher, one of the great ones. Nearing the entrance, a thought struck me and we drove back just in time to hear the woman doing exactly the same lines for Maher who dangled his mike at his side and whose camera was as discreet as a camera could be. Images of the Emmy disappeared as I saw this act was obviously well-rehearsed.

There were many other standout news stories: the assassination of Martin Luther King when the troops were on the streets again, and Lake Erie smashing into lakefront communities and washing around my feet as I stood there trying to do a story, soaked and shivering, and finding a houseful of people, in two feet of water, playing poker and refusing to leave.

Hell, I was such a dedicated soldier I even brown-bagged it for dinner each night. I took thirty minutes off to watch Walter Cronkite, and then started the whole drill again for the eleven o'clock report.

That expansive feeling—that anything was possible—was in the newsroom and present in us as well. That sense of camaraderie was there—we all just liked each other. Jac and I were doing well as a team; he was a bit more serious and maybe that was why we clicked the way we did. After about a year I came off street reporting; it was just too much with the six and eleven news shows, but I was still writing and editing all of it. Jac had other business interests at the time, and really wanted less responsibility rather than more. He pretty much stuck to anchoring.

Where did common sense, reason, and judgment figure into all of this? In a small quiet corner that I didn't pay much attention to. I only knew that I loved it, every crazy, driven, frenzied minute of it. I was really good—and we were annihilating the competition. But the hours and hard work exacted a heavy toll. My marriage was falling apart, and I was falling apart as well.

Maybe I was getting to be like an apple left out in the sun too long. I was beginning to dry out and I could feel it happening from the inside out.

Sometime in 1970, my marriage failed. Helen and I had separated for a while and then came back together. But we were not communicating. Things were not working out between us, but we never quite acknowledged what the problems were. We had three wonderful children. I think Helen was a good mother to them, and I think that I was a good father. But I was a lousy husband.

I think there was a restlessness on my part. Maybe it had something to do with the teen life I never had. After all, when most young men are out buying their first car and moving out of the house to gradually leave the nest and go on their own, I was dodging bullets on a beach in the Pacific. As soon as I got back to civilian life I went immediately into marriage, and then into another war. Who knows why things happen? A delayed adolescence maybe, or maybe just two people who grew apart. Our biggest mistake, I believe, was in trying to cover it up and pretend that it wasn't happening.

We spent so much time making the children believe that everything was peaches and cream and sugar and spice and good times for all. Underneath, it was falling apart and, perversely, I was doing nothing to help. In fact, I was working more and more. This business, with its incredible hours and enormous demands, could erode a saint. I was not a saint.

The station had become the focal point, the stage, the arena, for my life. Fifteen or twenty years ago, in that time of expanding local television news, the day-to-day demands were huge.

Ray Lane came on board for sports shortly thereafter, joining Van Patrick, a fabulous man who died eight years ago. Even before I was hired, Marilyn Turner was already at Channel Two, in a small way, as the Saturday weather woman. I was working Monday through Saturday, Jac was working Sunday through Friday, so Saturday was the one day a week that I anchored alone.

Weather forecasting was really just a sideline for Marilyn at the time. She was a freelancer without any major contract or commitment because she was doing other commercial work: TV commercials, photo and film work, even traveling to New York for national spots. The station talked with her about doing more shows, but she really wasn't interested in taking on anything that would lock her in.

Then we got this new kid, Jerry Hodak, for the weather. It was because of him that Jac and I and the Channel Two news team invented what's now referred to as Happy Talk. Happy Talk News refers to the relaxed atmosphere now famous in newsrooms where the coanchors and news team are free to interact and joke during the newscast.

Anyway, Dean McCarthy, our program director at the time, saw that the new kid was a little nervous and uptight. He suggested that we tease him a little bit to help make him feel comfortable and loosen up.

JERRY HODAK

I had really wanted to be a street reporter when I came to Channel Two. I had been in Orlando for four years doing TV there, but Detroit was home, my turf, and I felt that I belonged out on the Detroit streets. I was doing summer relief—for everyone—and the station promised me something would open up by fall.

Well, they really needed a weather person more than a street reporter. There had been a long history of "Miss Fairweathers," an apt name because none of them seemed to last too long. The weather was a complete package, its own segment with a little theme song and the news wrapped around. They had talked to Marilyn about it and she wasn't interested in doing any more than weekends, and there I was, an employee with a contract but without a slot.

I realize that I presented quite a change from the succession of weather women that preceded me. I was twenty-three, but looked about nineteen, and had a wardrobe that consisted of conservative blazers in subdued colors.

Besides, Sonny Eliot was doing weather on Channel Four. He was funny and enormously popular, a virtual one-man band on the air, and I didn't think that anyone could overtake him. But for all of his one-liners and inventive language ("frou-zy" for fair and partly cloudy for example), he didn't have anyone to interact with.

We figured we would have some fun with the situation until another Miss Fairweather came along. Besides, we had nothing to lose; at that time Channel Four dominated the ratings in the local news scene.

John and Jac were totally irreverent and without

mercy. They called me "Geraldine" and made fun of my blazers. I assumed it was all their idea, because it was entirely in keeping with their characters. There was John's laugh; he was always saying outrageous things and laughing about them afterward. Sitting around in the newsroom, he was just naturally funny. I found out later, much later, that the news director put them up to it. But they didn't need much encouragement.

During that first commercial break in our debut, one of the station managers at the time, Jay Watson, told us to get on with the show and cut out the bullshit. Within the first hour after we got off the air, the "bullshit" drew 400 phone calls into the station from the viewers at home. The folks at home didn't know what to make of it, but they knew we were having a good time.

To put it simply—we clicked. We didn't think of it as Happy Talk. We didn't have a name for it. But it was a decided break from tradition. Within thirty days, the station had stopped looking for another Miss Fairweather. They had their news team—with the human touch.

It all seems so primitive when I think back on it. We were in black and white until 1967, and for clouds, lightning, or the sun I'd use little magnets on a map. There were no such things as satellite photos or computers.

In those days, the ad boys would come down to the studio and we would rehearse the commercials, but not the weather. The sponsors were much more closely tied into the individual segments. One sponsor might pay for the 6:25 P.M. sports, for example, and Jac had a Standard Oil logo on his jacket each night.

I did commericals—*live*—every night and that

always provided us with plenty of spontaneity. For example, one time the ad agency had ordered me a beautiful white Stetson hat to wear for a commercial for the Dodge boys. Only nobody bothered to check my head size! As the hat settled down over my eyes and ears, John and Jac really went to town.

We also had a barbecue grill set up in the studio for Kowalski hot dogs. I was the chef in charge, and I also poured a glass of Stroh's beer each night for the benefit of our viewers. The trick was to get the head to come just to the top of the glass and not drip down the side—while looking directly into the camera. My hand was sure and my gaze was steady. We were not allowed to drink the stuff because we were on the air, but the stage crew was, and I endeared myself to all of them.

By 1967 we were broadcasting in color, and TV news was beginning to get serious. Reports from Viet Nam were beginning to surface, although they were not yet a regular staple in the daily lineup. The production end was beginning to become more sophisticated as well. We packed up the barbecue grills, got the anchors away from pitching products, and weaned the sponsors away from the segmented sponsorship of news, sports, and weather. Our Happy Talk gained a bit of refinement, more like a cocktail hour than a neighborhood picnic, but our chemistry was firmly in place and was working each night with the precision of a well-oiled machine.

But it was still before the days of writers and producers and major support staffs in the newsroom. John was doing everything, even the graphics. I guess there are just so many of those shows that people have in them, and the crazy hours do not help. We certainly were dominating the news scene—but there were long breaks between newscasts each night to while away in the newsroom. We'd joke, talk, share occasional dinners, and gossip. And I knew that John was getting burned out.

JOHN

My contract was coming up for renewal at Channel Two in 1972 and I knew one thing—I had to get out! I didn't know where or to what. I just couldn't stay and do what I had been doing. It was just too much. I was burned out.

I was still married, but I wasn't spending much time at home. In fact, at that point I wasn't sure what home was or what I wanted. Marilyn and I were good friends then. Just good friends. Did she add to my sense of confusion? Maybe.

That's where timing comes in. I guess I have had my share of good luck and happenstance in my life. You don't last in a "thirty seconds and cut" medium like television without some special intuitive sense of it. Anyway, I knew that things were out of whack, and that I needed a total change. I had moved out of the house, rented an apartment, and was ready to cut a blazing trail of fiery disaster behind me. Just then, I received a call from a Detroit attorney, Henry Baskin, a friend now, but only an acquaintance at that time. He told me Channel Seven was planning a morning talk show—7:00 A.M., five days a week—and they were looking for a host.

5
BAROMETRIC PRESSURE FALLING, STORM CLOUDS MOVING IN

❁

MARILYN

Would it be worth it? There was airfare, food, a hotel room for a week or so. I'd weigh the cost with the potential earnings. Generally, I would share a room, sometimes with as many as four other young women like myself. It took a while to get it all started, and I think I ultimately had much better luck in New York than in Chicago. Furthermore, I had the weekend weather job as a base of operations to fall back on. There were local commercial TV spots that had started coming my way, and modeling work with the auto shows as well. At five feet, two inches I was too short for fashion work, but I was proportioned just right for doing advertisements for the "Muscle Cars" of the early sixties.

By 1965, I think I was successful, independent, a career woman. Fortunately, it was before the days of local gossip columns. Columns like *Yours Truly, Darling,* and *Carol T.* were not yet operating in the local papers. I don't think the local press had started to realize the fact that their readership was interested in TV news personalities as personalities. In my opinion, those were good times! It certainly made it easier for my kids and for Bob and his practice.

I was establishing a very substantial career doing national commercial work. I appeared on many spots. Most people probably wouldn't even recognize me, as they changed the way I looked.

I think I might have spent as much as $2,000 each year on the trips and auditions. But the way I figured it, if I hit on just one commercial each year, I could make back seven or eight times that investment. A standard residual fee for one of those thirty-second spots was $14,000 to $17,000, and this was in the sixties.

For a good while, I was doing more than just one a year. My neighborhood friend from Windsor had given me the name of an agent in New York, Chuck Tranum. He was not a personal agent in the literal sense. He probably managed at least a hundred models at any time, like a stable of talent, making sure that you heard about auditions for your "type" as they came up.

I definitely had a "type" in those days. The "spokesperson" type of commercial that had been popularized on national TV spots in the fifties by women like Faye Emerson and Betty Furness was giving way to little true-to-life "situations" that required some acting skills. I was too short for a high fashion image, but I was just right, totally convincing, as the neat, energetic homemaker, the trim young mother, or the cool, efficient airline stewardess. I kept an extensive supply of shirtwaist dresses on hand and wore my hair in simple page-boy hairdos. That is what typical housewives wore. False eyelashes were quite fashionable then. I wore them, but carefully took them off and put them away before those auditions, because that was *not* what most typical housewives wore.

The way the procedure worked in those days was that I'd get a call at my home from Tranum's office about an upcoming audition. There would be a brief description of the product, the potential fee, the situation or story line, and what kinds of clothes to bring. Then I would decide—what were my chances? What would my investment of time and money be?

Once you tossed your hat in the ring, there could often be as many as 200 others starting out along with you at the first audition or "cattle call." One commercial I tried out for (and got!) was for Palmolive soap. There were 400 young women at the first audition. Some were from as far away as California, but for most auditions, the women trying out were from the area around New York.

It might take as many as six or eight auditions to narrow down the numbers and cast the commercial, and you certainly could figure out pretty quickly that there might be at least twenty other girls who were exactly right for the spot. We all felt the tension of competition.

There were usually about twenty other people that you had to please, from people from the ad agency to representatives from the corporation itself—be it Palmolive, Procter & Gamble, whatever—to the video production company. Of course, they each had something a little different in mind.

Another important factor was impressing the casting director, who would make the cuts at each round. This person was the official link with the ad agency at each audition; in the sixties the job was always filled by women, though I understand that is no longer the case. Furthermore, advertising people tend to be very mobile. They change job titles and agencies at a whim, and it was rare to see the same bunch more than once.

I was never confronted with any "casting couch" phenomenon while on those auditions in New York. I don't believe that I ever lost out on a national spot because I didn't sleep with someone. There were so many people involved with putting together each of those commercials, there was so much money riding on each product, that you would have to be sleeping with the whole city to use that method as your ticket. You couldn't count on just one person to get you through it.

That is not always the case, however, as I have observed in Detroit. At least one local TV news-weather job that I did not get, but that I was well qualified for, was won by the woman who was dating the program director at the time. I think the atmosphere at a local station is different. There is a closeness (sometimes too close) that develops when people are doing similar work day after day in the same place.

A commercial I did for Milk-Wave Lilt, a home permanent, featured a white set, white costume, and four white kittens; it got a write-up in the performing trade journal, *Variety*. I did a spot for Palmolive Liquid with "Madge, the manicurist," one of the earliest of the Madge series. Another spot that I did for Palmolive shampoo involved taking a shower for three days straight, standing behind a shower curtain in a bathing suit with lather in my hair. I appeared as a shirtwaisted Mom for a product called PDQ, a flavored drink much like Ovaltine. I had a young son who crashed through a brick wall whenever I called him for his PDQ.

Then there was a spot for Prell shampoo, with me dressed as an airline stewardess talking to a distinguished-looking gentleman in a three-piece suit on a plane. I still see him on national spots from time to time. He's timeless like Madge, who has got to be in her seventies by now. I did spots for Purina dog and cat food as well, again as the housewife in the shirtwaist and with a beautifully cooperative pet.

Sometimes, you'd hit at the audition and get the contract, but the product would strike out. I remember one product called Shield, an antiperspirant being developed by Procter & Gamble. The ad campaign featured me as a weather woman, of all things, dressed in cool whites and beiges to suggest staying cool and dry. Well, the product did not test well in its control areas in the South, where these products are typically tested, and the whole ad campaign was scrapped. I had about six months tied up in this advertising campaign for a product that never made it to the marketplace. I was paid for the work, but the promise was to become national spokeswoman for the product, which is every commercial announcer's dream. Jan Minor was a soap actress before she became spokesperson for Palmolive as Madge, and that became a lifetime career for her. But it didn't happen for Shield and Marilyn.

Back in Detroit, I had picked up a succession of local spots and some "regulars" as well. The spokeswoman type of commercial had never really lost favor on local spots, and I did food and furniture ads on a regular basis. They did not pay that well individually—forty dollars a spot, which really didn't compare to the work available in New York—

but I was doing from three to five of these per week. We would generally start taping at around 1:00 P.M. and finish by 4:00 P.M.

It was a great life. I never worked as hard, or as many hours, or had to get up as early in the morning as I do now. Working from job to job as a freelancer, I never had to take an assignment I didn't want to take, and I was always able to make money and keep busy.

Meanwhile, my marriage to Bob Turner was failing. It was apparent to me after a few years at Channel Two that the marriage was definitely moving on a different track from the career. We were two people, moving very fast and hard after two careers, and splitting off into very different directions. Again, that feeling overtook me—I was not going to "put up with things," and I had the financial means to do something about it.

Bob never liked television people, never wanted to associate with any of them socially, and was openly critical of them in every regard. He thought that he was smarter, that he could do it better. He thought he could do everything better. But the biggest problem became his moods. Quickly he could become surly or belligerent. Often, he would be cheerful, conversational, even pleasant with one or two drinks. Then he would keep on drinking, maybe one or two more, and get nasty and ugly.

As I began to see more possibilities for myself in a career, I think I wanted more concessions out of the marriage—and certainly more appreciation of my worth. One instance stands out in my mind now. I had wanted to have my front teeth capped for many years. There wasn't anything terribly wrong with them, but they stuck out a bit in profile shots.

I had been doing TV weather and photo work for

the auto shows at that point, and even in those early days I was brutally honest about my professional work. That includes how I look on camera. I don't think it is vain or superficial to think this way if television is your livelihood and your profession. And even then, I felt it was my profession and saw the possibilities it held for me.

I knew that my smile could look better. I found a dentist in New York who would make caps for me after several in Detroit turned me down because they didn't feel it was a serious enough problem. In the sixties, most physicians and dentists in this part of the country tended to be more conservative about the possibilities of cosmetic surgery or dentistry than they might be now.

It meant two trips to New York to have the dental work completed, one for the temporary caps, another for the permanent teeth. They were beautifully crafted out of porcelain by a Chinese ceramist who was a virtual artist at that sort of work.

I came home beaming—naturally. Only I got cold water thrown in my face. "They look dumb. I can't understand what you were so excited about," was the Bob Turner response.

The Marilyn Turner response? I was angry and hurt—again. Here I was making money with that smile, money that we were both sharing. It was a marriage and a medical career that I felt I had contributed to in equal measure. There should have been emotional support for *my* career, and it just wasn't there.

I believe to this day that I could have learned to live with Bob's cruel indifference to my career and feigned ignorance of the contribution I had made and was continuing to make. There was another problem, the biggest one of all. Bob was a drinker.

During the early days, when there was very little money, the drinking was confined to weekend beer drinking. But as time went by, and we left residency and Bob entered practice in Dearborn, the drinking increased. He moved from beer to gin to vodka. And it wasn't weekends—it was every night. Four to six drinks in an evening were routine. After one or two, he became relaxed, very pleasant, and good to be near. But I learned the hard way that after a few more drinks, he became abusive. At first, it was only verbal, and I could handle myself there. Later, it became physical. He would grab me by an arm and shake me about. Or shove me against a wall or to the floor. I would fight back, but he was six feet two inches and weighed about 200 pounds. It was an uneven match.

I'm not going to go into any more detail. This is still painful to talk about. Then, I didn't talk about it at all. No one—no one—knew anything about the drinking and the violence. I kept it to myself. There came a night following a terrible scene, when I sat up until dawn. That's when I reached the most difficult decision of my life. I was going to file for divorce immediately. I was young, I could support myself and my sons, and I could no longer live with half a life—good friends and honest appreciation on the outside, while inside my home an abusive husband, my closet secret.

SYLVIA STRAITH

Quite frankly, I didn't like Bob Turner. I didn't like the way he treated Marilyn. Very often he put her down publicly. Actually, it was rotten treatment. She worked to put him through medical school. She was the high school glamour girl and he was a football

JOHN

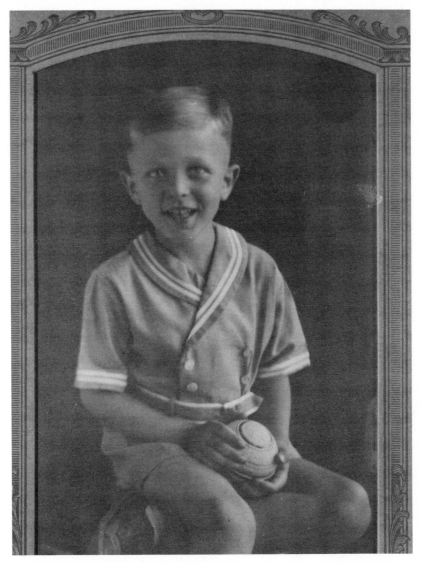

My mother always called me Jackie. Here I was out of hightop shoes so I must have been at least five.

(Top) *These are my brothers Kenneth and Daniel with me in the late thirties. Kenneth appears to have an itch.* (Bottom) *Eighth grade safety patrol, Woerner school, St. Louis. I'm fourth from the left, rear row.*

Here I am at boot camp, 1944. I was barely seventeen.

In 1949, I did a stint in summer theater on Cape Cod. Here I am in costume for "The Hasty Heart."

My first broadcast (college 1948), "Hannibal–La Grange on the air. KHMO, 10-70 on your dial!" I'm seated at the table on the left.

The sailor is home on leave. This is my dad, my mother, and the girl they always wanted me to marry.

WTVO, Rockford, Illinois— when I had nothing else to do, I was a goof!

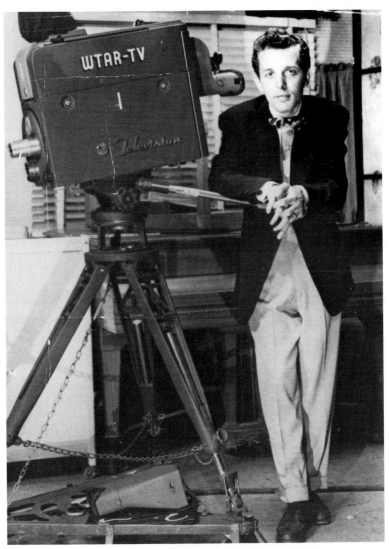

My first TV job, Norfolk, Virginia. Note the turned-up cuffs—I must have thought I was Gene Kelly.

Management! My first office, 1953. I was about twenty-six or twenty-seven.

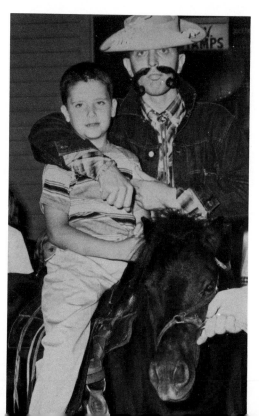

Rough and Ready Cactus Jack on WTVO in Rockford in the late fifties. Great mustache, eh?

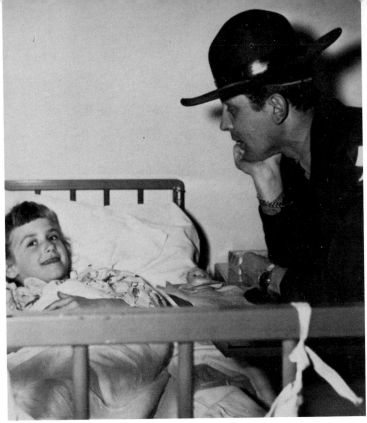

Here I am as Ranger Jim in Lansing in the early sixties. It was a children's show, and we visited kids in hospitals regularly.

My three terrific kids (1959), Kathy, Terri, and Johnny.

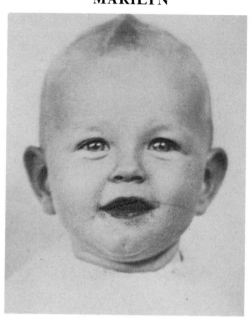

(Top left)*My mother, Evelyn Cousins, when she was six years old. 1910, Pelee Island, Ontario.* (Top right) *Baby Marilyn. The hairsylist had an easy job.* (Bottom left) *Here I am at eight years old—one of the pudgy years—Barrie, Ontario.* (Bottom right) *A budding accordionist at eleven years old, 1942.*

Here I am at fifteen going to my first prom.

A wife and a mother at twenty. Here I am with my first born, Robert Ross Turner.

Four generations of my family: me, my grandmother, Bertha Mae Cousins with Rob on her lap, and Mother.

My first commercial (1955) was for Wishing Well Soda at CFPL-TV in London, Ontario.

My first photo-modeling composite done sometime in the mid-fifties.

The resident obstetrician-gynecologists' picnic. Bob Turner is in the back row, far left, holding Dean. I'm in the front row, seated at the far right, with Rob at my feet.

Rob and Dean on the ice in Dearborn. I was a hockey mother on the sidelines for years.

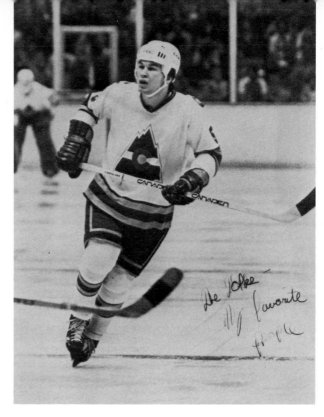

Dean went on to professional hockey. Here, with the lamented Colorado Rockies, with whom he scored his first NHL goal.

Rob lives in Fort Myers, Florida. Here he is with his doberman, Garbo.

My debut as Miss Fairweather,
WJBK, Channel 2.

Me and the rest of the "Miss
Fairweathers" in the late fifties. The
women were not even given names.

At WXYZ, the weather was sponsored by Drewry's Beer. Looks
like typical Michigan weather.

*This ad appeared in the early
seventies—a lot more than a pretty
face.*

*The number one news team in town in 1974.
We're all still around (except Troy Dungan,
who's now at a station in Texas).*

*An ad campaign in the mid-seventies. Bill Bonds had gone to WABC in
New York. The main team was Kelly, Jac LeGoff, Al Ackerman, and
Turner. Jac and Al are now at WDIV.*

This is the first "Kelly & Company," fall 1972. Marilyn wasn't on this one. She was still doing weather and commercials on Channel 2. With me is newscaster Mary Ann Maskery, now Far East correspondent for NBC News.

It wasn't discussed on TV but the forecast is wedding bells for John Kelly and Marilyn Turner

TV love story
Channel 7's Kelly, Turner to marry

By JAMES GRAHAM
News Staff Writer

Wearing dark glasses and clutching a $5 application fee, TV news star John Kelly strode into the Oakland County clerk's office yesterday to obtain a license to marry his weathercasting sidekick, Marilyn Turner.

The WXYZ-TV (Channel 7) news anchorman, recognized despite the glasses, later confirmed, he had, indeed, applied for a marriage license in Pontiac.

The admission by the newscaster put to rest one of the media's favorite guessing games in recent weeks.

Kelly and Miss Turner had been dating for several months but neither would con-

firm wedding plans.

Reached later, Kelly refused to say where or when the wedding will take place.

"We've located a relatively private place for the ceremony and don't want that messed up," he said.

He also refused further comment on his wedding plans, remarking, "I'm exercising my right to privacy."

Kelly appeared alone at about 11:30 a.m. yesterday in the clerk's office to pay the license fee and fill out the marriage license application form.

He listed his name as John William Kelin Jr., 47, of Southfield. He listed his bride-to-be as Marilyn Patricia Turner, 43, of Bloomfield Hills.

Kelly listed his occupation as "newscaster," while listing Miss Turner's job as "television announcer."

Kelly was at WJBK-TV (Channel 2) as a newscaster for seven years before jumping to Channel 7 in July, 1972, to host a morning talk show. He joined the station's news team — where Miss Turner was already a regular — in January, 1973.

Miss Turner had been at Channel 2 as a part-time newscaster and weather forecaster for 12 years before going to Channel 7 in September, 1972.

Kelly has been married once before and has two daughters and a son. Miss Turner has been married twice before to the same man and has two sons.

The article from the front page of The Detroit News *the day after we got married.*

hero, and after they matured a little bit, possibly they didn't have quite as much in common. She was in a completely different class. In later years he was verbally abusive and physically abusive. I saw the bruises. But Marilyn was very old-fashioned. She had a straightlaced upbringing, and I think that made her accept a lot. I suspect her first thoughts were you just didn't get out; you didn't divorce. I think Bob loved Marilyn, but he kind of wanted to put her on a shelf and take her off when he wanted to do something with her.

MARILYN

Is there more marital instability and divorce in this business than there is in others? Probably. The pressures are very great, and it takes a certain kind of drive and ambition within the individual to stick with it, through the ups and downs and rejections that are an inevitable part of it. The fame and the notoriety that come with success also have a bearing on it. Oftentimes a spouse cannot understand it, and jealousy develops. If the couple makes it through the lean years, and suddenly one partner gets all of the glory, that is one kind of problem. Then there is the problem of the struggle; some couples never stay together through that. Either way, one partner is bound to feel left out. It takes an enormously large ego and sense of confidence not to.

Another problem is the hours and the schedules. Television is not a nine-to-five kind of life—for anyone. On weekdays when we are doing the show, John and I go to sleep by nine o'clock. We have to— John gets up at half past four each morning because he likes to do certain things to get ready before each show, like reading a couple of newspapers. I get up

75

a bit later. I study my material for each show in the morning, starting at around a quarter past five, and I leave for the station at ten past seven. Think of the commotion that could create in a family if one spouse was living this way and the other had a nine-to-five job.

I had pushed for the divorce. Bob was definitely opposed to the whole idea. It was bitter and difficult, and the kids struggled with it. I really don't think there is ever a time to get divorced when you can avoid some of the problems that affect children. I think that their suffering over the first divorce was one factor in my decision to try to put the marriage back together again, six years later. I had been working and contributing financially to the marriage, so was I not awarded overly generous child support. I feel I was almost penalized for being an equal partner in the marriage—I never thought the settlement was adequate.

The single life, the second time around, was a much different state of affairs than at age nineteen. At first I dated a lawyer, and then some businessmen. There was a rumor that spread around that I was seeing Jerry Cavanaugh, who was Detroit's mayor at the time. That was totally untrue and unfounded. He evidently heard it as well, and called me at one time to find out if I had any notion of how it got started. We had a good laugh over it, but that was as far as that ever got. I can't help thinking that, today that kind of rumor would keep the *News* or *Free Press* going for *months*. Later, Jerry Cavanaugh married a lovely blonde, after seeing her for some time. Obviously, there was enough similarity for some people to confuse her with me.

I did have a relationship with a man who was

about ten years younger than me, long before that particular variety of May-December relationship was in fashion. Again, I was ahead of my time. The young man was twenty-six years old, an intern physician at one of the Detroit hospitals at the time. He saw my picture in a Detroit talent book and called the station rather persistently, wanting to meet me. I was apprehensive; it certainly seemed bizarre, and I figured that he would undoubtedly be weird. Finally, I agreed to meet him for coffee at the station.

He definitely was not weird. Quite the opposite, he was a very charming, sensitive young man. His looks reminded me of a very dark Michael Caine. The relationship began to develop, and at first I was so embarrassed about the difference in our ages that I didn't tell anyone. But we became very involved, to the point of considering marriage. It wouldn't have worked in the long run, though. At first, he felt he wouldn't mind not having children, and I, in my mid-thirties by this point, was not interested in having any more. There was a religious difference too, which at first he felt would not matter. The more we talked, the more we both realized that the issues of *his* potential children and *his* religion did matter—a great deal. It was a tearful parting, but a wise one.

He married very quickly after we broke up. I have seen him since, a few years ago in Florida where he settled. He is enormously successful in his work as a neurologist and has two children.

For the most part, I never felt that the single life was so exciting or glamorous. There are no ground rules, particularly after you have been married and are in the working world. One day you want someone to mean something to you, and the next day, there is no one to mean anything. For me, I saw it as a situation of highs and lows with many more lows than highs.

Certain things are different for young working women today than they were in my day. For example, two of our producers on the show took off for a vacation together on the French Riviera for two weeks. I never thought of doing things like that. I never felt quite that carefree. But then, by the time I could afford it, I had two children. I guess I didn't use my situation to its utmost. Damn it!

Of course, in a situation where there is a divorce, the father of the kids is never totally out of the picture. Also, Bob Turner was never the sort of person who could be easily ignored. Bob would go along for a while being cooperative, then suddenly fall behind in his support payments. I'd have to get the lawyers, and the bitterness and belligerence would start up again. He remarried briefly during that time, and flexed his muscles in other ways to try to hurt me. And I still cared enough for him so that he could.

An opportunity had come along that I very much wanted, as a national spokesperson for General Foods. I was aiming for such a situation, one product that I could work for and be identified with in a consistent way. I had heard about a young man in New York who was doing the ads for Marlboro, working about twelve days a year and making $450,000. And that was in the sixties.

General Foods would have offered me this kind of opportunity. It would have been a big contract with me as representative for all of their food products, TV, print ads, and personal appearances as well. It also would have meant that I would have had to move to New York. I tried out, tried out, tried out again, and it got down to the wire. It was between me and one other girl.

I lost out on it—and I was heartbroken because I had gotten so close. But perhaps it was best in the long run. I know that I would have had problems with our custody arrangements. Bob had stipulated that I could not take the boys out of the state of Michigan, and I probably would have had to give up my custody rights or get into an ugly confrontation.

EILEEN TURNER

Marilyn and Bob and I were in Las Vegas for the second marriage, and I stood up for them. Marilyn's parents were not there. They were opposed to the reunion and had gone to Spain for a vacation. She planned the wedding for the time that they would be gone because she knew how they felt about things.

We were all sitting around the hotel pool before the ceremony. It was a beautiful sunny day, and Marilyn and Bob were debating: "Well, should we enjoy the sunshine, or should we get married?"

I thought to myself, "Well, if that's the kind of decision it's going to be—don't do it."

I don't think it was cynicism on their parts. I think they were both very scared. They had been apart for six years when they decided to remarry. They knew what it was like without one another and they had each had a lot of pain in the process.

MARILYN

After almost six years of being single, working regularly, raising two boys, and living in a very fine downtown Detroit apartment, generally living a single life, I reached a point where it seemed as if it would go on forever. That didn't make me happy. Throughout this time, my sons, Dean and Rob, saw their father regularly. I would see him when he'd pick up the boys for the weekend and speak to him on the telephone. Those conversations were not always pleasant. On the other hand, many times they were. Cautiously friendly is a good way to put it. One day he called to say he was picking up the children and by the way he was getting a divorce. Soon after that the calls became more frequent; we had husband-and-wife conversations. Should he buy a certain piece of furniture or why didn't I have lunch with him? I helped with the furniture and had lunch with him. During this time, I was in counseling, and once I spoke of possibly marrying Bob again. My counselor said that if I was thinking of remarriage, it was perhaps best to marry that which I knew rather than entering strange territory. And me—I believe now that all of my background supported marriage, that you married, had children, and lived together forever. When Bob asked me to try it with him again, I did. I talked it over with the boys. Dean, just eleven years old, had always hated the idea of divorce. He wanted a mom and dad at home like everybody else. He was wild with happiness at the thought.

Rob was different. When I talked with him, he looked at me and said quietly, "It's never going to work. It didn't work the first time. What makes you think it will work the second time? It will never work."

Wise words from a sixteen-year-old. And I listened. He said things that scared me. Two years later, he was proved right. Nothing had changed, and I knew I had to escape Bob Turner. What a wrenching, terrible thing to put those boys through—again. When we remarried, Bob promised to stop drinking, and for a while he did. But he began again, and it was worse than ever. There was one terrible night of drinking and violence, which I do not wish to detail, other than saying Rob was threatened with a pitchfork and I was dragged down a staircase by my ankles. I called the police—they never came.

How could I have been so wrong? I filed for divorce and moved out after the divorce was final.

EILEEN TURNER

It was wrong, all wrong. Marilyn was not prepared to put up with things the second time that she wouldn't take the first. As for Bob, I think he really loved her. He had tried desperately to find someone to take her place. He tried harder than anyone else I know to be happy. After their marriage failed, he became terribly bitter, and he felt that my friendship with Marilyn was disloyal to him. I actually did stop seeing Marilyn at that time—but only briefly—because he felt so strongly. He was having a hard time of it. He had suffered a serious heart attack and had a nearly fatal car accident during the year after as well. But the worst pill came when he heard that John Kelly had filed for divorce. Bobby was a sad person after that, and a self-destructive one.

He seemed intent on destroying himself. He married again, I think just because he knew what was going to happen and he wanted to beat John and Marilyn to the altar.

Marilyn and I have been, and remain, close to one another. Part of the reason has been John. He has always been super to me, and I have always felt welcome in their house. But mostly it is Marilyn.

There is an honesty and an electricity about her that is unique. She is a grand total of six months older than me, yet, when I am with Marilyn, I always feel young.

MARILYN'S MOTHER

I was disappointed when Marilyn married Bob Turner. She wasn't able to complete her university studies and instead switched and got a teacher's certificate. She had to help support him, even after Rob was born. They struggled along. Later in their lives together I knew that he drank heavily, and that was a thorn in her side. But when it came, the divorce was the first in our family, and it was a great disappointment to have a small family shattered. And I always felt the second marriage was going to happen. She wrote me a letter about remarrying Bob. It came so swiftly that her father and I were in Spain, and the letter never caught up with us. So when we got home, she was married again.

Marilyn could never have been just a mother and housewife; she would have felt she was losing out on some part of her life. Not that she wasn't good at home, but she was always interested in entertaining people. When she was five or six, she'd get a "concert" together with her friends and charge fifteen cents admission. I suppose I could be accused of being a stage mother in a way, but I never pushed her. She was doing the things she wanted to do, and I gave her all of the advantages I could. So there were dancing lessons and music and, of course, skating. She had such drive. Looking back at it now, I wonder how I ever kept up with her.

Material things never mattered that much to

Marilyn. I can remember picking her up after school and telling her we were going to buy a new dress, and she'd say, "I don't need another one, Mother." Even today, she's very practical about the money she spends and is not extravagant. And she never seemed to envy others. Well, maybe she is extravagant with animals. She was always interested in them. I have an old snapshot of her sitting in a little wagon with a toy Boston terrier. She didn't have her own real dog until she was sixteen. We surprised her—she was blindfolded, and we handed her a cocker spaniel puppy. She was wild with excitement and had that dog for years. She still talks about him.

Marilyn has always been considerate of me, a loving daughter to her parents, and she is a good mother. I've been proud of all the things in which she's been successful. I think John balances her out in many ways. He's not as impulsive, while she jumps to conclusions. John *is* quick-tempered, but he weighs things. He needs her, too, and depends on her. Possibly he doesn't admit it, but she's a good influence on him.

Robert Turner, M.D., suffered a fatal heart attack on April 8, 1975. Survivors included his third wife, Joan, two sons from his previous marriage to Marilyn Turner, and a seven-week-old daughter, Kelly. He was forty-seven years old.

6
WE GOT WHO YOU WANTED—AND A CAST OF THOUSANDS BESIDES

❧

JOHN

So in 1972, I went to Channel Seven. I got a morning show, my *own* morning show, seven o'clock to half past eight, with stars on promotion tours, authors on book tours, interviews on the issues of the day—the whole shot. The format was not too much different from our present "Kelly & Company," but there was one notable exception—we did not have a live audience. We changed its name from "AM Detroit" to "Kelly & Company," and we used my ideas about the way it should be. In other words, no regulars, as I felt that they weighed things down and became a crutch. Oh, we had a few people who made frequent appearances, but we did issues, a lot of issue-oriented interviews. The newsman still lurked within me and sent out strong signals to the outside world.

One issue that was hot at that time—those years

soon after so many American cities had rioted—was gun control. We had several shows dealing with various aspects of that issue, and on one particular show where I had Della Reese as a guest, we spent an hour looking over this whole arsenal of guns that the Detroit Police Department had confiscated and brought in.

Because that first morning talk show was on in an earlier time slot than our present "Kelly & Company," it was harder to get as many big-name guests to come into Detroit. So, although the dieting and exercise craze wasn't as much in vogue as it is now, we did a lot of interviews on health-related subjects, and sports figures were a regular staple.

The show was followed by Rita Bell's "Prize Movie." That was fine with me. I have never been a Rita Bell fan, and that was to become very evident a few years down the road. But at that time, her morning movie show had a big following, and that sort of combination kept the viewers riveted to one channel.

I don't remember too much more about it, probably because it didn't last much longer than that. Within six months, my long-awaited talk show was yesterday's news.

The first hint came innocently enough. Our general manager, Jim Osborne, invited me out to lunch with Channel Seven News Director Phil Nye for company. I thought this was strange since my contract was with programming, not news, and *what the hell was the news director raving about me for anyway?*

The little bells that had started ringing in my head were turning into a dull roar by the second lunch date. The morning show—my morning show—was in jeopardy. There was a big morning operation on the drawing board, which later became "Good Morning America," and the network was very anxious for it to succeed. "Maybe we can schedule your morning show after the network's morning show," went the tone of the speculations that seemed to have a decisively pointed underlying message to them.

"But we'd really like you to do the news." That was the nitty-gritty, and Nye and Osborne, finally, came through directly, loud-and-clear, no mixed messages on that subject.

No one knew where morning programming was going in 1972–73. "Today" on NBC had been the only long-running network show. CBS had not come up with its morning program, and ABC was just thinking about getting into the running. News on the other hand was *hot*, nationally and locally produced.

However, I had scrupulously avoided the Channel Seven newsroom during my brief months at the station, and I was openly critical about it. I disliked everything about Channel Seven news: the set, the look, the approach, the weather, and I disliked the way Bill Bonds did the news besides. He had already developed a reputation and had gone through a couple of coanchors by that time. One in particular, a fellow named Barney Morris, was someone whom I liked a great deal, though it was well-known that he had a serious drinking problem, even in those days.

Another Bill Bonds casualty was a valued friend from my days in Peoria, Jack McCarthy. In 1966, I suggested that Jack take a job that was offered to him as a street reporter in Detroit. I was anchoring then and recommended him to the company. Jack was a terrific newsman and a good writer. Jack left Channel Two to coanchor with Bonds after Barney's departure, but Jack didn't last long. He may not have been anchorman material, but Bill ripped through him.

I realize now that a good deal of my feelings were due to the burnout I had experienced in the crazy years at Channel Two. Also, there was the matter of my life, which I was trying desperately to get in order.

I wanted Marilyn Turner. It was just as simple as that. And as complicated. When she had gone back to her husband Bob to try again, I must say that I was jealous. But on the other hand, we became better friends and I felt more comfortable with her afterward. It was as if some of the emotional pressure that was drawing me into her life was gone.

Saturday nights were lighter in the newsroom. I didn't work on Sundays, so there were no assignments to make for the next day. We'd go out for supper between the six and the eleven o'clock shows. Sometimes we'd go out with one or more of our sons, so there would be four of us, or six of us, or three, or just the two of us. That didn't change after she remarried, and I was grateful for that.

JERRY HODAK

I don't know why—but I've always understood that there are diabolical minds at work out there. I was happy for John when he got the offer of the morning show at Channel Seven. It was a better contract, with more money, and he was intent on changing his life around.

But I had a gut feeling about it. Those guys in management at Seven wouldn't have cared if he'd wanted to do a kids' show. They just wanted to break up the team at Two. I told John at the time, "Six months from now, you'll be back doing the news."

And my prediction, or apprehension, turned out to be accurate.

JOHN KELLY

You take a good hard look at the competition, the product. Only in this business the product happens to be people. The local talk show, my talk show, was only going to be a filler until the network's show could be put on the air. I had two choices: like it or not, I could adapt gracefully and go quietly off to the Channel Seven newsroom, or I could let them take me in bits and pieces, whittling the talk show down to an hour, or half an hour, playing around with the scheduling, and the like. That is ultimately what the station did after I left the show. Dennis Wholey, who later went on to achieve national exposure with "LateNight America" on PBS, took over the morning show at Channel Seven after "Good Morning America" was in place in the 7:00 A.M. slot, and it was down to thirty minutes when he left it.

I had become a victim of the dirty tricks that I had come to know so well on the other side of the fence, as a short-lived program director in Atlanta.

My attorney Hank Baskin observed, correctly, that Channel Seven's management really wanted to put this anchor combination together. He also kept telling me that there was more money in doing news, and that, as long as I was satisfied to go that route, he would get the best possible contract for me.

That was what we did. We had to negotiate a new contract, with news department instead of programming. Baskin drove a hard bargain. I got a three-year contract with lots of escalator clauses, overseas assignments, and domestic assignments, so I could move around.

BILL BONDS

The guys in management—they bring you in because you've been successful in doing what you have been doing. Which is being a newsman and performing it day after day. The moment they get you hooked they say, "Don't do what you've been hired to do. Do what *we* want you to do."

And most of these people who do the hiring don't know the first thing about how to be a good newsman.

Look what happened here in 1972. Our general manager at the time, Jim Osborne, took a look at Kelly and Le Goff on Channel Two and saw that they worked well together. Jac always ended the newscast with a kicker, no matter what, and John always laughed. And the camera closed with a close-up of John laughing.

Now Jim Osborne says: "We want him. What is more, we want to break that up."

That was the theme of the ad campaign—"We Got Who You Wanted." But once they got him and paid a bundle of money for him, they wanted to change him. Now, John was in his forties and had been around in this business. Give the guy a little credit. Who knows John better than John?

MARILYN

It was just luck and timing. I had decided that I wasn't going to go back to New York for any more auditions. I had the weekend weather and the modeling jobs and regular commercials that turned up around Detroit plus a lot of little things. I figured that something would come along. And it did.

Within a month after I had made that decision, Channel Seven became interested in having me do the weather five days a week, at six and eleven. News Director Phil Nye and V.P. and General Manager Don Keck made the offer. Actually, they approached John about it and asked him to ask me if I wanted to make the switch.

I pretended that I wasn't that interested, but in reality, I was thrilled. Now we were talking about absolutely steady money. I got Henry Baskin to help with the contract, and we drove a very hard bargain.

The money was not as great as you might imagine. I think it was in the range of $35,000 to $40,000 a year, but the anchormen were making $150,000, even then. The big issue of negotiation was that I was able to continue doing commercials on the side. Management didn't like it, and they tried to stop that. They've tried since, too, but they could never stop me from doing commercials.

Al Ackerman and I started on the same day in November 1973. So there we were, all of the shinning lights that had been gathered from all of Detroit's news teams into one colossal pot.

JOHN KELLY

Channel Seven had a full house. They were ready to go all the way to promote us.

We all went to Chicago to film an absolutely masterful ad campaign. The biggest thrust was on TV, but it was a full media campaign with newspapers, billboards, bus ads, and radio. There was an enormously creative series of thirty-second TV spots, all tying in with the print ad theme. It was done by that advertising whiz Joe Seidelmaier, who later went on to develop Wendy's Restaurants' "Where's the Beef?" campaign a few years later.

For Channel Seven, he dreamed up these two Laurel and Hardy types in trench coats who were kidnapping each of the four of us: Bill Bonds, Marilyn Turner, Al Ackerman, and me. There was this little situation with these two shady characters, and the ad would conclude with all of us turning up together, safe, smiling, and eager at Seven.

Bill was nabbed out of a movie theater. Seidelmaier shot his own western scene for the purpose, and Bill was watching it on the screen when these two guys nabbed him.

I was whisked out of an elevator. First you'd see me with my dog, then the two henchmen would get in, and the door would close. It would open, but only the dog was left.

Marilyn was taken from a phone booth, which turned out to be a sedan chair. She was whisked away while she was absorbed in conversation—in other words talking her head off (so she didn't notice). Al was stolen out of ringside at a prize fight.

The point was that the station was prepared to spend mucho dollars to become Number One. And within the year after I started doing the news with Bill, we accomplished that.

BILL BONDS

Somebody has to be the main person, the captain of the ship. I have tried to explain this to Jeanne Findlater, our present general manager. "Jeanne," I'd say, "there couldn't be two general managers of the station here at Seven. There can only be one, like it or not. And it's the same way with anchoring."

The eleven o'clock news cooks in this town. It's good on Two, it's good on Four. The reason we're all good is because it's very competitive. Detroit's a helluva news town. It's ethnic, it's industrial, it's technological, it's sophisticated, while simultaneously blue collar.

I was anchoring here and John was doing the morning show. I had known him before, met him when he was street reporter at Channel Two and I was a street reporter at Seven. I knew Marilyn, too; I met her at a dance when I was still a disc jockey for Keener 13 radio. I always loved Marilyn. I mean, I have known Marilyn a long time and I've even had fights with Marilyn. I have had fights with John, too, over the years. But it's much more fun to make up with Marilyn.

Anyway, this was an ABC-owned and operated station, and a hot-shot flashy kind of guy named Al Primo was president of ABC News in New York at the time. He had come up with this concept of EYEWITNESS NEWS, machine-gun style readings of the news. No more than twenty seconds without visual backups, each segment no more than ninety seconds with visuals. It had become very successful in New York and San Francisco. Jim Osborne, our general manager at Channel Seven before Jeanne Findlater, got wind of it. Unfortunately, so did Channel Two and they stole the name EYEWITNESS NEWS right out from under us. Jim Osborne got Al Primo to Detroit, got the four of us together, and said, "We think you and John would be a great combination."

John had been doing a morning talk show on Seven, but it didn't last more than about six months.

He and I got together over a couple of dinners at the Vineyards, and John said he would do a nightly news coanchor on a fifty-fifty basis.

I said, "What does that mean?"

He said, "That means I'll lead one show and you'll lead the other. You could do the next, and I'll do the next."

So we did it for five years until I was offered a job in New York.

JERRY HODAK

First of all, Bill Bonds is a very territorial kind of guy, kind of like a lion who is king of the jungle. You know that he had to be wondering what all of these people from Two and Four—Kelly, Turner, and Ackerman—were doing on his turf.

There was one-upsmanship all the way. It surfaced almost immediately over the issue of commentaries. Neither Bill nor John has what you would call "modest" egos, and both of them thought they were the world's greatest writers. Bill did commentaries, and he poured his heart and soul into those commentaries. John didn't believe in commentaries, but it didn't take him long to figure out that this was too intense a cause with Bill, and too powerful a weapon to ignore. Finally, John started doing commentaries.

What had really started to happen, though, was that local news had become very popular, and the revenues generated from it started to grow. It became an issue of economics. The station that could capture the larger audience share could sell its ad spots for a higher rate and would have a head start on prime-time viewers in the bargain. In the days before TV viewers had remote controls on their sets, that audience might keep that same station on their dial through the eleven o'clock news into the early morning show.

Every story you have ever heard about John sitting on two pillows because Bill sat on one pillow is true and then some. John and Jac at Channel Two were a comfortable fit, like a pair of well-worn shoes. Suddenly, here were these two strong characters, literally attacking the camera. Management is always going to try to build the anchors at a station. That's the seat that everyone wants, with or without pillows.

Besides, I always stand up for my spot at the weather board.

BILL BONDS

I never particularly liked John's lead stories because, first of all, I had always done the lead stories. I think Jac Le Goff led the show at Channel Two, and John would do the second show and close with his famous laugh. He had played second banana to Le Goff for many years, at least that was my understanding. He wanted to change that at Seven.

So you've got four different people. Al Ackerman had three and one-half minutes of sports, Marilyn's got three minutes of weather, John's got thirteen to fourteen minutes of news, and you want to do your best. I mean, there's John saying I want to look good, sound good, and be good. Or Al—I want to look good, be good, and sound good. Or Marilyn—I want to look good, be good, sound good. Everyone is primed up.

Sometimes, I'd say, "Hey, we don't need three minutes of weather tonight, John."

"Wait, Bill. It's not just weather. It's Marilyn doing weather."

I would never put myself in that position again.

95

Now on the other hand, I love Marilyn. I've had a secret crush on her for years. I mean, you look at this woman, and say, "Gee, I'm attracted to that."

John's an Irishman, and he likes to laugh. He likes to tell jokes. People saw the contrast between the two of us immediately and tried to make bad chemistry out of it. It takes a long time, particularly in a major market such as Detroit, to establish a personality, or a combination, over the air. This is true nationally as well. Look how long it took NBC to get the Bryant Gumbel/Jane Pauley combination running smoothly. They weren't good together at first. CBS *still* hasn't got its morning show running exactly the way it wants it.

There is an instant recognition factor that happens to all of us in this business, John, Marilyn, and me. I've been recognized in Mexico, Madrid, and Los Angeles. People come up and say, "Aren't you Bill Bonds? We remember watching you doing the news in New York," or "Didn't you do the news in L.A. a while ago?" Once I was on an island in the Caribbean, in a gift shop, wearing nothing but a pair of shorts, and some folks came up to me to say, "Hi Bill, we've watched you do the news each night for ten years."

Is there anything in life that can prepare you for that kind of exposure, for that kind of *personality*— to be **A** Bill Bonds, **A** John Kelly, **A** Marilyn Turner? I don't think so.

HARVEY GERSIN (*V.P., Reymer & Gersin, national media consultants with headquarters in suburban Detroit.*)

Our company has been in existence for fifteen years; I've been involved with it for ten. In the early sixties, it became evident that news could be a profit center.

You could increase ratings, revenue, and audience competition.

My partner, Arnold Reymer, worked for McHugh & Hoffmann, one of the earliest TV consulting firms, which started out in Detroit back in the sixties. It has since moved to Washington, D.C. That company, which was the first in this business; Magid and Associates, which is based in Cedar Rapids, Iowa; and ours, here in Detroit, are the three largest in this business. Detroit has a good airport, so it is no problem to be located here. We work for stations all over the country and have clients in Detroit, though I'd rather not say which ones because we consider confidentiality an important part of our business.

In 1976 when I joined Arnold Reymer, we had eight employees and five clients. Ten years later, we have 95 employees and 135 clients, which include the whole range of electronic media: TV, radio, cable, independents, teletex, videotex.

Numbers matter in all sorts of ways in our business. You can assume from those numbers that there was a need in the marketplace for our services. Obviously, television is the sort of medium where you have to communicate in a way that is quick and interesting. The pictures have to match the words, and the personalities have to mesh as well. Call it chemistry, whatever. But there is much more than just electronics.

What we don't do is run anybody's stations. Much of our work is research-based. We have developed sampling techniques, and we study viewer psychology. Based on that, we develop a strategy for our client—appearance of the set, writing, special content, features, interrelationship of talent on the set. We can provide a talent coach to work with on-the-air personalities; we can develop an on-the-air style.

We use Watts lines, focus groups, or personal at-home interviewing to sample opinions. From these we write up an analysis and present it to the station's key production and management people.

Quite often we get called in to consult when a station wants to move from third place to first. But then again, some stations don't want to be Number One. It costs too much. Number Two can often be very fine and very profitable. But some stations will spend anything it takes. And it takes time and chemistry. If people feel or look uncomfortable, the viewer can sense it.

In a big market like Detroit, all the stations have big staffs, and they can all cover the big stories. Presentation style and the people on the air—the talent—become more important. It becomes a business of little tiny advantages.

Some newscasters have a great deal of skill in asking questions. Newscasts are generally very structured, very formatted. Some newscasters just cannot make that transition from highly structured news to a less formatted talk show. Being able to ask a question and then *listen* for the answer is a great skill. In the medium to smaller markets, the on-the-air personalities have a lot to do with the preparation of the newscast. In the bigger markets, there are staffs to do that for them. In a market the size of Detroit, anchorpeople now have very little to do besides commentaries. It's not very difficult. The program is pretty heavily formatted. Anchorpeople just have to read with a commanding style.

JERRY HODAK

Nielsen was no good, too superficial—just age, numbers, and sex. Consultants could give you the *whole* story. At least that was management's reasoning.

And they would go out on street corners, or call on the phone to sample people's opinions. They'd come up with a presentation to management such as: 17,000 women between the ages of eighteen and forty-five are watching so and so. There were a lot of management guys who were weak and indecisive. And many people in the business were uncertain about the direction of the news.

The consultants created a position for themselves. A few managers bought their surveys and studied them, but made their own decisions. But many, particularly in medium-sized markets, put a lot of faith in what consultants had to say, to the point of tailoring feature items to suit these surveys.

JOHN KELLY

Near the end of my stint at Channel Two, I became aware of the existence of a new category of media—consultants. They were starting to analyze the news, particularly the local news shows in other markets.

Suddenly, at Two, we were starting to hear a lot of "mentions" about the nightly local news show at KGO, San Francisco. It was "machine-gun" news. The maximum length for one news item without film support was twenty seconds, film stories went a maximum length of ninety seconds. It ultimately became the style that Channel Seven adopted.

Once I got to Channel Seven in the seventies, they were embroiled in this all-out effort to be Number One. The consultants were having a field day. At one point, New York had brought in three different consulting firms to do analyses for this station. Worse yet, these guys are self-perpetuating. They usually come with a three-year contract, and they find enough to criticize so you have to keep them around to implement the misguided notions that they have started.

None of us were ever privy to any of the information that consultants came up with—except what management wished to share. Later that information found its targets, Marilyn and me, with machine-gun accuracy.

But in 1972, 1973, and 1974, all was starting to seem right with the world, or righter than it had been for the few years before.

7
JOHN AND MARILYN TOGETHER AT LAST

JOHN

When I moved to Channel Seven, I also moved out of my house and took an apartment in the Franklin Towers. The marriage was not right and couldn't go on, but I couldn't bring myself to end it, either.

I had become estranged from my family, no doubt about that. By lifestyle and habit, I don't think I am a man-about-town, but slowly, I had become a "night person." That goes with the job. There's this adrenaline that pumps through you when you always have a deadline. Every night after I got off the air, I'd be home within fifteen minutes to a half an hour, but I could never get to sleep right away. Helen hadn't seemed able to adjust to that. I felt that she should have been able to be there once in a while when I came home—just for me. She couldn't make herself stay awake that late—even on Friday nights.

So I always had lots of friends outside the TV station, because I didn't want to face an empty house with no one there for me. I also had lots of hobbies: flying small aircraft at Pontiac Airport, and horseback riding at Hell Creek Ranch. Several guys, Bill Combe, salesman, pilot musician, and the wittiest man I've ever known, and Larry Adams, now an M.D., then owner and operator of Oakland Aviation, and singer-comedian Bob Posch were good buddies. They were always ready to go at a moment's notice.

There was an active nighttime scene of local clubs in the Detroit area at that time, and I got to be a well-known figure at many of them. A couple of terrific entertainers, namely Josh White, Jr., Jack Brokenshaw, jazz vibraphonist, pianist Matt Michaels, and Bob Posch were always appearing in one club or another. I'd drop in, often on a Friday night after the 11 o'clock news, still feeling revved up and raring to go, and would often wind up joining them onstage for a little bit of improvised "show business."

But there was the matter of my family, my kids, and my own attitudes, which had been planted deep down in the soil of the Kellys and Kelins many, many decades before.

JOHN'S MOTHER

John's father and I were very disappointed when his marriage broke up. I know they tried to work things out; they just couldn't seem to communicate. I'll never really know all of the reasons, because he never talked with us about it. It would surprise people to know—those who see him on television—that he really is a very private person and finds it difficult to open up about many things. I'm sure I'll be surprised by what I read in this book! Still, his younger brother Daniel is a minister, and I know that John talked this situation over with him. I've wondered if it wasn't missing his teenage years while in the navy; he seemed so much older when he was discharged. Yet the navy made him more considerate and very thoughtful of us. He talked with his dad quite often, then he'd go off and do what he thought best anyway. He was married at just nineteen, but I was married at eighteen and have stayed that way for sixty-one years.

His family is proud of him. We're scattered all over the country in four different states. We all know that if we need help, all we've got to do is say the word, and he's there.

MARILYN

I know this sounds corny to say, but John and I had a real brother-sister act before the relationship became a romantic one. I've said before that you should be friends first, lovers second, and I believe that was the way it went for us. We started seeing each other in a different light somewhere between the two divorces. But it started and grew more intense, I believe, because of the things we had in common from our working together. Even so, we didn't marry until two years after his divorce.

JOHN'S MOTHER

I first met Marilyn a few months before they were married. She was a bit more sophisticated than I, which made it difficult for me to understand her. She'd been out in the world, working, while I've led a fairly sheltered life. Don't misunderstand; we have a good relationship. I think she's made John a very good wife. He's a fortunate man—a *very* fortunate man—in having had two good women to love him. He and Marilyn work so beautifully together; each is receptive to the other's ideas. And he has a temper—just like me that way—flare up one minute and the next it's under control.

JOHN

I had thought for some time that marriage with Marilyn was probably a good idea, but I suspect the idea was considered with the typical male vagueness many protest doesn't exist, but in certain matters definitely does. So we discussed the possibility. It was going to take place. We were definitely in love and even grateful to have found each other. The actual plans took hold during the early part of the 1974 football season. In those days John Laffrey, proprietor of Laffreys Steak House at Eight Mile Road and Telegraph, organized what he called "Football Parties" for every home Lions game. It was a complete package: gather at the Steak House for a pregame brunch, buses to Tiger Stadium, and of course, seats for the game, then back to the Steak House for dinner and entertainment until closing. So it was at one of these, at the postgame dinner with a group of friends, that the pinning-down of a wedding date began. Somehow, it almost seemed like a committee meeting looking for a majority decision. At one point, I recall Marilyn saying, "I think December the twenty-seventh would be a perfect time."

"Ah," said old pal Billy Combe (himself a bachelor at the time), "the old one-two two-seven play, eh?" And suddenly it was set. Laffrey insisted on "doing" the wedding (if he could be flower girl, but later declining the honor), and another friend, Jerry Mickowski, said he'd do flowers and "stuff." (Stuff turned out to be gorgeous and included candelabra, runners, you name it.) Laffrey even had a location in mind and not only arranged a wonderful feast, but booked a band for dancing.

And so the deed was all but done.

Of course, it wasn't all that simple. For instance, Marilyn—with typical pessimism combined with a dearly romantic soul—took pen in hand and designed a truly magnificent medallion as her wedding gift to me. It was intended to be worn around the neck on a matching chain. That was the romantic part. On the back of the medallion, she had engraved the following:

FOREVER
December 27 1974

Forever what? Forever anything, she said. Can't trust an Irishman until you've got him pinned and locked, she said. I've always gently joshed her by trying to get her to admit she worked out a generic marriage medal. "Of course," she replies in a withering tone. And those feelings were truly deep in both of us. We had bombed out before; could this really be right?

So far, so very, very good.

MARILYN

John Laffrey and Jerry Mickowski did a marvelous job. It was the loveliest wedding and greatest party I've ever attended. Even if it was ours.

John had just concluded an arrangement with the county to manage Addison Oaks, a far Oakland

County estate that had been in the Ford-Buell families, we were given to understand. The wedding took place there. We had chosen not to send out invitations, because we wanted to make it as private as possible with no press attention. So we invited our friends by word of mouth only. But still, within a very short time it became public knowledge, more or less. As a matter of fact, it became a media event. But some lovely things came of it. A young man running a limousine service offered a free Rolls-Royce for the wedding. We accepted, of course. The Somerset Inn management gave us a suite for the wedding night, prior to departing for our Jamaican honeymoon. I'll always remember arriving there at about three in the morning, dead tired, to discover lovely flowers and still-cold champagne from the management.

JOHN

We used a small room at Addison Oaks, with a roaring fireplace, candles, and dim lights, as a chapel for the wedding itself, with only family and close friends in attendance. Billy Combe was my best man; Marilyn's lifelong close friend, Sylvia Straith, her matron of honor. The black-robed minister stood in front of the fire, the wedding party facing him. (We learned later the poor man thought he would melt from the fireplace blaze.) Things went well until Billy, to my right and slightly behind me, spotted Sylvia beginning to cry. That did it. He released a gulp, sniff, and quavering deep sigh. That, in turn, was all I needed to begin to go. Marilyn, gusher always at the ready, noted that I was beginning to barely contain myself, and her tears began to trickle, then flow, and she was barely restraining sobs. Oh, it was a joyous affair!

It proved impossible to stay out of the limelight. The press crashed the party. Obviously, the time between Christmas and New Year's Day is a down news time, with not much going on, so we were splashed all over the front pages. It resembled a presidential news conference. And the reception line and personal picture-taking went on for hours.

What a party. Great food, drink, dancing, and a great, *great* time.

All our guests enjoyed themselves, but none, I think, as much as Bob Talbert and Henry Baskin—and our family, sons, daughter, and parents. I carry the vivid memory to this day of Henry Baskin, normally a contained man—as the crowd was thinning and Marilyn and I were beginning to prepare our escape into the night in the royal Rolls-Royce—climbing over the bar in search of a touch more champagne. I think he felt that his months-long work on me, including sending me into self-supporting bachelorhood, had worked, and he was celebrating!

MARILYN

Seven months later—after all of that—we separated.

I believe the problems we had stemmed from the fact that John couldn't get over the idea that he had gotten a divorce. In his mind, you had one wife and one marriage! Never mind if you cheated on her every now and then. Suddenly, he found himself married to a different woman. We waited two years, and I had hoped it would give him enough time. But I guess he wasn't ready, and we probably should have waited even longer than that.

Meanwhile, we were still doing the nightly news and the weather while all of this was going on. Can you imagine? All of that frost going between us, and here we were on the air, with him introducing me each night.

JOHN

To this day I don't know what possessed me. How can you describe a separation that took place over a decade ago? Today, we're different people. Yet, the high points of the thing (or low points) seem very fresh. For the life of me, I don't know what triggered it. Obviously, after barely a year of marriage, neither of us really knew the other all that well. But I was definitely the instigator, the dealer in melodrama, if you will. I do know that very late one night I simply walked out, climbed in my car, and left.

There was a great deal of driving, and many pit stops for coffee. The last was at a doughnut shop on Orchard Lake Road as dawn broke. From there, I drove to our attorney Henry Baskin's house. The poor sleepy man pulled himself together and made more coffee, strong and bitter, and in his kindness had my nerves jangling like a convention of Swiss bell ringers. After what seemed like hours of patient listening to whatever jumbled burbles were coming from me, he began to talk. It was not a lecture, it was understanding. It became clear that he felt his old pal John was being foolish, that Marilyn was very special and worth doing just about anything to keep, and that I should take immediate steps to repair this breach, if possible. By this time the caffeine had worn off, and I was nodding off. Hank was kind enough to put me to bed in his spare bedroom.

When I was rested and awake, he continued to counsel me with general and practical advice. I don't know if there were clandestine calls to Marilyn or not, but I do know I was stubborn. I asked if I could stay with him a week or so. He needed a house guest as badly as he needed a third eye, but of course he agreed, wanting to keep me under observation. I shocked him a couple of days later by showing up with a closet full of clothes.

I had gone home to Farmington Hills to get them. Marilyn was there. I can see now that I really wanted to repair it all right there, but didn't find a way through my stiff and misguided pride to get the words out. At this point, Marilyn's pride and honor, always prickly at best, were outraged, and she *certainly* was not going to do it. So there was stony silence as I humped piles and heaps of clothing to the car and rammed them in, all the while getting increasingly agitated and edgy. What I *will* always remember is Marilyn standing at the door, wearing a dark robe and arms folded, saying quietly as I made what turned out to be my last trip to the car, "John, you're a fool." That did it of course. That did it for almost a year.

Instead of a week, I was with Baskin for a month. Now, understand, the man was a bachelor and had finally purchased a house on which he had just completed phase one of redecorating. He enjoyed his house. He entertained. Friends came and went, many of them female.

Meanwhile, I was a tortured man. Remember that Marilyn and I had to continue to work together at six and eleven every evening, Monday through Friday. It was stony silence, for the most part. In one respect, we were lucky in that the newsroom and weather office, while on the same floor, were separated by the length of a central corridor. No face-to-face collisions, or anything like it. When on the air, she was in and out of the studio for the weather while I sat like a lump for thirty minutes. A lump acutely conscious of her presence. Never, *never,* try the happy talk news format with a wife from whom you've chosen to separate. She did it as only she can, with great aplomb. She was absolutely magnificent. I, on the other hand, was a great clomping marble-mouthed clod.

For a time, the station was unaware of the separation. But not Baskin. Through the month I hung around, he gently and not-so-gently tried to persuade me to give up my asinine position. No success at all. Finally, in desperation, he told me he knew of a place I could rent—a condo. Further, I could do it on a month-to-month basis. Poor man. I'm sure if I had stayed freeloading for another week, he would have paid my rent and maybe half the furniture. I was not a fun person to have around.

So I moved into a bachelor pad. I lived in it for seven months in absolute filth and disorder. My own state of mind was pretty disordered too.

Through a late fall, into winter, spring, and summer, Marilyn was in the house in Farmington Hills; I was in a condo in Royal Oak. I rented furniture, buying only those things you cannot rent: dishes, minimal silverware and cooking implements, towels, sheets, and the famous bedspread. I reasoned that if I bought a heavy enough bedspread, I wouldn't need blankets. So without further thought and because I didn't take time to shop and in complete ignorance of what really was available, I bought a bedspread. It was white and long-haired and weighed about two hundred pounds. If I lay on my back, I couldn't straighten my toes because of the weight. If I threw it off, I'd wind up balled into a freezing knot. Many is the night I wound up under an overcoat.

Finally, about six months into this madness, I realized the magnitude of the error I had made. How to get Marilyn back? How can she forgive me? What can I do? There were so many mornings I greeted after a wide-awake, tortured night trying to sleep.

What it was, was loneliness. I wanted my wife. *Again*, Hank Baskin helped. Over the months, he came at me from various angles, and he was pretty subtle. From him I learned the bachelor life wasn't all that great, that good women were hard to find, that Marilyn was good at this, great at that, fine at something else, and, gradually, it took effect. I finally realized and admitted to myself that Marilyn was the one for me. Period.

One of the things that solidified my thinking was a discovery. I noted earlier that we . . . the news team . . . usually were out of the station at about 11:45 P.M. or so. While Marilyn and I were acutely aware of each other . . . we never spoke aside from the on-air necessities. And that included departure from the station. Occasionally I wound up driving out the gates just behind her, which (I think) was only coincidence.

One night I noted to my utter shock that instead of turning to the left on Ten Mile Road—the way home—she was turning to the *right*! She wasn't going to Windsor to visit her mother and father at that hour! I was stunned. She was seeing someone else.

MARILYN

After three months of the separation, the marriage apparently over, I finally announced to Dean, "Marilyn Turner is coming out of her cocoon. I will no longer remain locked in my tower like Rapunzel."

This was not a sudden decision. For weeks, after the word about our separation had begun to seep out, I had been getting calls from various mothers who thought their recently divorced sons and I should console each other, and girlfriends who knew just the guy for me.

JOHN

All this, of course, I figured out later. All I knew then was that she was indeed seeing others and beginning to enjoy herself. Living another and hopefully better life. And for Dean, the only son still living at home, the atmosphere had undoubtedly improved.

I was devastated. For weeks, I vacillated between wanting to punish her (she, of course, didn't know or care) and plotting to get her back.

Finally, not all at once, we got to the point where we were talking again. I began to engage Marilyn in conversation. I wrote notes. I escorted her to Bob Talbert's wedding. In short, I began a campaign, even though I did not recognize it as such.

Spring came, and I learned that Marilyn had reopened our cottage at Lake Shannon, near Fenton. One Saturday morning, at the end of a riding lesson and without even leaving the saddle, I called her and somehow she agreed to a visit. I think I went from the horse to my car in one jump. I headed out in boots, britches, and jacket. It was the first friendly conversation, and it took place on the deck of the cottage as she lay in the sun. I recall she even grudgingly told me I looked good. I thought maybe I'd wear the boots, britches, and jacket for the rest of the week.

Gradually, the thaw began.

Marilyn's always liked jocks, so one Sunday when I was competing in a dressage event, I took a chance and asked her to come. I don't think that I have that rugged macho image she gets turned on by. But that Sunday, with me in control of the horse, I must have conveyed some of that. Anyway, I was in costume: shined black boots, tight tan britches, blue blazer, white shirt, black tie. We did a little circus stuff, and I ended the routine with the horse in a bow.

Marilyn liked the way I looked in my outfit. We talked, at first like two circling dogs eyeing each other. Eventually we went for drinks at a nearby Troy bar, where I thirstily quaffed beer and desperately tried to further my cause.

Although I think she had already made up her mind when I asked if she would let me try again, I was ordered to wait for a few days. I then was told a trial reconciliation was going to be allowed. Marilyn, Dean, and a friend of his moved me from the condo back home a few days later.

Despite the enormous pressures of the public life we lead, including nearly four years of two shows a day, it's working. And I'm grateful.

DEAN TURNER

Mom's had her ups and downs. She's jumped from station to station and has had a lot of personal controversy. There was a lot of action going on in her personal life in the early seventies after the second divorce. It could give nightly "Action News" a run for its money. Sometimes, I find myself scrambling to remember it all.

But she's a survivor, and she's always had this attitude that she would land on her feet. And she has. That confidence has helped her enormously. I think she has always been able to get more work, in spite of the uncertainties in this business, because her attitude is so strong.

A lot of people recognize me in my own right because I have played professional hockey for five years. But when I was playing in Little League teams through high school, I'd get a lot of razzing on the ice. People would yell things like, "Oh, Marilyn's little boy," or "Your mother should play hockey, not you," or "Your mom's as bad on TV as you are on the ice." I probably got more of that as I got older, and as my mom was getting more air time from doing the five-day-a-week weather. I always felt that goes with the territory.

My mom went to all of my games, especially all of the Little League stuff. Occasionally I'd go down to Channel Two, and later Channel Seven, with her for her weather broadcast. I remember I had this set of junior encyclopedias, and I'd usually cart one along in case I got bored.

I was always aware that she and John were good friends. I knew that they had always been fond of each other. But I was a young kid, and I guess you don't think about those things. I was more concerned with my fastball and the fact that I was tetherball champion of my elementary school. Those were my major concerns. I guess kids can be very selfish that way.

My dad and my mom cared very deeply for one another for a long time, but they couldn't seem to make it work. You can't always identify a certain event and label it, but you can feel the tension. I think that was what I felt when their marriage started coming apart. I was about eight or nine when things had become particularly rocky between my parents. I used to think, "What the hell's goin' on here? I'm going to be the star pitcher on my Little League team next year. I don't want to move from Franklin to Southfield, or Southfield to Dearborn."

But I never felt sorry for myself. I think I was included in many things that many kids don't get in on. Because most of the socializing Mom and I did was with adults, I always felt comfortable in the adult world. There were several times I would go along to Chicago when my mom would go for auditions. We'd drive in for a day or two, and I'd walk along with her until she'd go in for the call to read her lines.

I'd always stay up and watch her do the weather. When I was very young and she was doing the weekends, I'd wonder whether she could watch me too, through the TV set. She'd joke about it. "Yeah, I was watching you. You were sitting around in your underwear!"

Usually I'd stay home when Mom would go on auditions to New York. Either my grandparents would come from Windsor or I would stay with the live-in maid. The rules of the house would break down pretty quickly if it was the maid who was in charge. First of all, I'd usually get all of the cookies I wanted. One maid, Eunice, had a seance in the house, candles all over the place, while my mom was gone. Mom came home and couldn't figure out why there was wax all over the house. Eunice got fired once my mom got the pieces all put together.

I was particularly rough on my mom during that time after the second divorce. I had wanted her and Dad to get back together—pushed for it, campaigned for it. It was wrong for both of them though, and when they got the second divorce, I testified in court

115

and announced that I wanted to live with my dad. I really became very distant from her for about two years.

I was about thirteen or fourteen at the time, and any young man at that age looks at his father as something really special. I felt, "He's my dad. He knows everything—whatever he says is just fine!" When I look back on it now, I resent the fact that he used me the way he did.

Maybe my dad came from another generation where he wasn't used to a very aggressive, strong, ambitious woman, and my mom is no shrinking violet. He was terribly jealous; he'd become enraged when anyone paid a lot of attention to Mom.

Later, this jealousy became focused on John Kelly. After John and my mom got married, it would drive Dad crazy. You couldn't put Channel Seven on when he was around.

I think Dad had his own personal problems that went back much further than my mom. They all came to the surface those last couple of years after their second divorce. He had a second heart attack. Then we were in a terrible car accident just as he was getting back in shape. He hadn't even resumed work when it happened. He had just come back from California where he had gone through something called "water therapy."

We were together in Chatham, Ontario, where I had played in a hockey tournament. It was an awful night. The roads were icy and slick, and we skidded right off and into a utility pole. The car was practically ripped in two, and he was badly mangled up. Miraculously, I was unhurt. I dragged him out and gave him a nitroglycerine pill under his tongue, because I was afraid that he might have another heart attack. I didn't sleep for three days after the whole experience.

His injuries were serious, multiple fractures, and he needed his spleen removed. The hospital called my mom. They had already been divorced for a year or so, but she was the only next-of-kin the hospital could find. She gave permission for the surgery and visited him afterward.

He seemed kind of confused, kind of lost, and very sad toward the end of those last few years. He got married again, for the fourth time, again in Las Vegas. He always got married in Las Vegas. He just called me on the phone and announced that he'd gotten married. I felt pretty pissed and said, "Well, thanks for letting me know."

There's no doubt in my mind that he just took life too seriously. He really ran himself right into the ground. I think he might have been going a little nutsy at the end. Just two weeks before he died, he was sitting at home and telling me that he had never loved another woman like he loved my mom, and here he was with a new young wife and baby. The idea of naming that new baby "Kelly" when he was so insanely jealous of John seemed particularly weird. Just think, her name was Kelly Turner.

I think that there was a time when I resented John Kelly, especially in the beginning. But I have always gotten along pretty well with him. As for the time that they separated so soon after they had gotten married, well, I guess I just watched and held my breath. I was sixteen and still living at home. My main concern? Well, like I said, kids can be very selfish. I just wanted to make sure my mom was going to get along OK.

ROB TURNER

There's about six years' difference between my brother and me. I'm older. When big changes in our lives were taking place, I maybe was more aware than Dean—or in a different way, anyhow. Earlier, I thought television was just Mom's job. But in junior high school I thought it was pretty great that Marilyn Turner was my mother. It bugged me when other people would say, "You're Marilyn's son." I'd say, "No, she's my mother." It made me more self-sufficient, though; I learned how to iron shirts fast. She was a step ahead of her time, and she learned how to handle the pressure. And when she was gone a long time, she had a housekeeper, and if I got out of line, *she* had a switch, and she would use it. Besides, there were sports to keep me busy. I was at football practice, then hockey practice—there were always enough parents around to hitch rides. My dad was always active because he was an ex-jock himself.

That all ended when I was about sixteen. They were divorced. I don't think it bothered me. It happened in Dearborn, and she took us and moved out. She was a new wave woman—she was aggressive. Later we lived downtown, and out of necessity I stopped playing hockey. I couldn't get to practice, so I gave up sports completely and concentrated on music. And I was getting to the age where girls started looking good. Mom talks about Dad's drinking, but I don't recall that—but she saw the demons and the outrageous behavior. Later, they married again. I remember telling her she was crazy to do it. Dad and I didn't get along until I was over twenty-one. I was a basement musician, and he automatically thought I was doing drugs. He was pushing my brother into sports, and I was out of it. Not in good standing with him. Anyway, she said, "Do you think I should marry Dad again?" and I told her I really didn't think so. But she did it; she did it for my brother. But it was a mistake. My dad was somewhat abusive. They had their spats. After their second divorce, when she and John were married and Dad died, I was hit with the fact that I was written out of the will, and my brother was written out of the will. The last time I saw him, there seemed to be no dissatisfaction with me on his part—he was pretty well self-centered.

Now, as far as I can see, I think John and Mom's marriage is great. They complement each other. I live in Florida now, but for three years I watched "Kelly & Company," and it looks good for both of them. At first I didn't like him at all because he wasn't Dad. That's natural; he's not an athlete. But he does athletic stuff, or did. He rides horses now. He likes to read. I hate to read, except the newspaper. Back then we had nothing really in common, but as time went on I learned, and I like him a lot. I have a lot of respect for him. And I've said so on many occasions.

Mom's best qualities, I think, are her love of animals and her personal drive. When she wants to do something, she doesn't do it half-assed. She's taught me about animals—they've become a big part of my life.

But she's headstrong. Sometimes she thinks she knows what is right, and even if you give her proof, she'll go on thinking she's right. And she won't listen. Then the same thing that's her good quality can backfire and be her bad quality. But John's happy with my mom. John's passive. He's really the one who runs the show, but he lets my mom think she does. They complement each other pretty well.

JOHN III

I was about fifteen when my dad and mom divorced. I would be lying if I said it didn't have an effect. I used to wonder about how I reacted, though. My

sister Terri—she's the youngest—went off the deep
end. My sister Kathy was married within two minutes, it seemed. But me—it was just like water rolling
off my back. One of the things that bothered me the
most was how it affected my mother. It was tough for
her. She had to be reminded of it all the time. In a
more conventional life you can start to get it over,
pick up the pieces. And what made it worse was that
when he remarried, it was someone in the business,
and they subsequently had a TV show together that
made their marriage one of the central parts of the
show. To this day, she's unable to completely avoid
it.

I suspect Marilyn thinks I dislike her, but that's
not true. She's my father's new wife. When I was
little, I was friends with Dean, and I spent the
weekend with him, so she was always this nice lady
and friend of my father's. I already had a pretty fair
relationship with her, and suddenly everything was
topsy-turvy. But I never held her responsible for
breaking up the marriage—she wasn't a homewreck-
er. Maybe it's something I'm still grappling with.

With the unexpected divorce, things were goofy,
weird. I don't think Dad anticipated divorce, and
he's always been there for me. My own mess-ups
with my life have seen him there to bail me out. He's
always been there for me. He's been a good father.

One thing I realized early about television: you
sacrifice your privacy. I remember going to a ball
game with Dad, and this usher came up to us and
started telling him a joke, a racial joke that wasn't
clear until the punch line, and I wanted to crawl
under the chair. I know Dad wanted to tell him to go
to hell, but he just smiled politely and turned away.

I'm in the business now, as a newswriter. I work
the worst shift and probably will forever, so I don't
think being John Kelly's son has given me any

special status. I'm more cynical of TV people than people on the outside. Some people that are in front of the camera need to be at the center of attention; they become egos out of control. Others have told me that my dad has dealt with it better than others, that he is still doing a job and doesn't run amok like others.

He wasn't heavy on advice about the business, other than encouragement. He told me not to worry because I could write better than others in the pit. And his level of success is rare—I admire that.

KATHY WANGLER

I guess I was in the sixth grade before I fully understood what my father did—that he was on TV. But even then, to us kids, it was just Dad's job. I never thought about it much. It was just Dad's job, and he had odd hours, and we didn't get to see him much. So mostly we did stuff with my mother, and we did stuff with my dad. I've lived up north for eight years now, and nobody knows him up here.

I was sixteen when my mother and father were divorced, and they didn't talk about it, only when Dad announced it. It was about the time when I was going with the guy I later married, and that gave me someone to talk to. Dad was with me and my brother and sister whenever he could be, I think. And later, when he and Marilyn got married, my new husband and I went to their wedding. We were the only ones who did—not Johnny and Terri. Marilyn isn't much like my mother. She likes animals, and I really don't know her very well. She's nice, she has been here. And she loves my dad, and that's good.

I always remember my dad being a soft touch. He still is with my daughter, Melissa. He would magically make candy and bubble gum appear for us when we were little. Really, my dad's just a nice guy.

JOHN KELLY

All the world loves a lover, and so it seemed, at least briefly at Seven during the months before our wedding. There had been a rule at ABC-owned stations, namely those in Detroit, New York, Chicago, Los Angeles, and San Francisco, that people who worked in the same department could not get married.

When we finally told them our plans, management checked it all out with Dick O'Leary in New York, the president of the five ABC-owned stations. He was a great guy, with that true element of Irish humor that makes for instant soul-mates. His verdict: "I only hope that when you get married, you do it during a ratings period and I can dance on the news desk!"

I suppose I was reasonably happy with things. I had the marriage that I wanted and, after all, even if there were the stresses, strains, and personality clashes of life in the newsroom, "Channel Seven Action News" was garnering all of the ratings and killing all of the competition.

Marilyn and I had a blissful honeymoon in Jamaica for two weeks, and then back to living and working. There was a new town house in Bloomfield Hills to think about, the ratings period coming up—and the consultants.

Machine-gun news? Well, Marilyn was the first to face the firing squad.

MARILYN TURNER

Here we were, Number One, with Bonds, Kelly, Ackerman, and Turner making it happen. After three years of this success, the station decided that they had to get new advisors. Now these people had to change something, or why were they picked in the first place? Right?

They did a survey and decided that the woman who did the weather wasn't credible enough. I had a little bit more time on my contract, so management put me doing this little fluff spot, "People in the News," about ninety seconds at six o'clock five days a week, which would take me to the end of my contract.

They covered themselves nicely, however, as they always do. They hired Jerry Hodak and told him that I wanted to do other things. And they let that story leak out to the newspapers as well.

In part, it was true. I had started a women's clothing store with another woman and was anxious to see it take off.

But if the whole situation were to happen today, I probably would have sued. We were Number One— and Turner was part of it and helped put them there. I felt it was discriminatory.

John was part of it too, but they were just as ready to let the axe fall on him.

JOHN KELLY

I was hurt. I was angry!

Jeanne Findlater had called me into her office for a meeting.

8
ENTER—DETROIT'S NUMBER ONE RATED TALK SHOW

JEANNE FINDLATER

I don't know if John is uncomfortable with its being said that I called him into my office and told him our consultants said he had "a laugh problem" and it was costing us ratings. That is true, but there are other things I said that John sometimes chooses to forget. I felt he was less essential in the news at that moment than in earlier days, and he was of more value to us in a morning talk show.

Besides, we had some new "players" at the station who were waiting in the wings. Doris Biscoe had been a street reporter at the station for a while and was ready to do more, and Diana Lewis, who had come from Philadelphia and had received a bit of notoriety from her brief appearance as a street reporter in the first *Rocky* movie, was only doing one news show a day. We were anxious to make spots for them.

Choosing one or the other, someone else could do the news, but there was no one else who could do "Kelly & Company." It was an easy choice for me.

JOHN

Jeanne Findlater was still new to the job of general manager when this series of events took place. She called me in—it was not unusual to have her call me in for an informal meeting—and I suspected nothing out of the ordinary when she did. There was no reason to be suspicious. Channel Seven Action News was Number One in the ratings and had been that way for a long while. There was no other competition at Two or Four to pose any threat to us. To this day, I don't know exactly what the consultants' report actually said. "Talent" is privy only to what "management" chooses to tell. I always suspected that the decision that my "laugh" was causing problems for my image, and problems for the nightly news' ratings, came from some gray, shadowy figure sandwiched somewhere in the layers of management in New York, or, more likely, the mysterious consultants.

But I got the message loud and clear. Management was going to replace me at the eleven o'clock news. I wasn't going to get fired or get my contract paid off. But I couldn't hope to perpetuate the status quo either. Jeanne told me I could finish out my contract, which had about a year to run, but she held out nothing for me after the expiration of that contract.

What to do? I managed to keep my swelling sense of outrage from rupturing completely into a full-scale explosion until I could hear the rest of Jeanne's plans during that first meeting. She made mention of the station's morning talk show. Dennis Wholey was doing it at that point, and it had been cut down to thirty minutes. His contract was running out, and he was going to be leaving the area.

The station was prepared to restore the ninety-minute time slot, though I realized within the next few months that they had an ulterior motive for being so compliant. There were a couple of tough negotiations to be ironed out.

I wanted the name "Kelly & Company" to be restored from "A.M. Detroit," and this turned out to be very complicated. I don't think that the station wanted to put up a fuss about this concession, and they recognized the benefits of this instant recognition, but the guys in New York felt differently. It seemed that wherever the network owned and operated stations, they had a morning show, "A.M. New York," "A.M. San Francisco," "A.M. Los Angeles," etc., and they wanted to keep the consistency.

Within a matter of a few weeks, however, Jeanne had convinced the powers that be in New York programming of the wisdom of the name switch.

Another important point of negotiation was the issue of the news. I would keep one foot planted in that camp by keeping my anchor spot on the six o'clock news. I had spent too many years in the newsroom, edited too many film stories, and looked at too many wire service reports to give that identity up. Certainly not then, and not with this bomb having been dropped on me. I was adamant about maintaining my place and credibility as a newsman.

MARILYN

So it was a peace offering. What's more, I suspected from the very beginning that it wasn't going to be entirely John's show.

127

I opened my dress shop, "Marilyn Turner's," in 1977, just at the time the new "Kelly & Company" was being planned. There were problems with my store right from the beginning. I had a partner who decided about four months after we got the store opened that she didn't want to be in the retail business after all. Besides that, we hadn't picked our location very wisely. We had considered putting the store in one of two suburban shopping malls, either Applegate Square on Northwestern Highway or in the Winchester Mall in Rochester. I chose the latter. Big mistake!

Unfortunately, it proved to be a dead mall without the kind of foot traffic or the kind of sales that we were counting on. So things were chaotic.

But I remember one thing all too well. When John came home with a press release for the new "Kelly & Company," right in front was a biography of Rita Bell and what she would be doing on the show.

I said to him, "You are not going to have this show all to yourself. This is going to be her show, too. This is going to be a cohost show."

John said I didn't know what I was talking about, that management had assured him that this was going to be his show. But I instinctively knew that management had picked Rita for it. She had a contract with the station that had yet to expire. Besides, she had been around for a long time and had a devoted following of fans for her "Prize Movie" each morning. And she had her supporters among management too, for they figured that a talk show would be a carryover from the movie hosting she was doing. She could take a few phone calls from viewers during the show too, just as she had been doing during the "Prize Movie."

Anything she could add to the program would bring added viewers, and, my God, the show had no track record! They didn't know what else to do with her, and it had a certain kind of logic.

JOHN

Management had another reason for incorporating Rita into the show. "Kelly & Company" was going to take a ninety-minute timeslot because Seven was doing away with "Prize Movie." The station hadn't purchased any new movie packages in several years and was running out of movies. These packages are put together by movie syndicators. They set the price for these packages based on experience and station advertising rates, but the fees are highly negotiable. So all of those issues came together at one time.

But there was one fly in management's ointment— or in reality, three flies: my attorney Henry Baskin; Channel Seven's executive producer, a virtual program genius named Bob Woodruff; and me. We wanted Marilyn to cohost the show.

Marilyn was a natural for it. She's a talker, a conversationalist, and interested in everything. I knew that she was right for an interview situation. Her face, her expressiveness would transfer well on television.

There were problems with Marilyn here, too, mainly Jeanne. It wasn't that she didn't want Marilyn. She did see our logic, but, for some reason, she didn't want to let Rita go. She became a champion for Rita's cause. She kept on talking to me of abstractions. Loyalty was one, for Rita had been at the station for twenty years, and Jeanne seemed particularly sensitive on Rita's behalf. OK, I could go along with that. But the other abstraction nearly drove me up the wall. She felt that Rita was so cute. And that was the rub.

Rita was cute all right, but she was out of sync with the times if she thought she could get away with that approach in an interview situation. It certainly wasn't the right stuff for contemporary talk shows in the seventies.

Just as the events of the 1960s such as the big-city riots, the Viet Nam War, the political assassinations, and the civil rights movement affected the nature of television news coverage, programs like "Sixty Minutes," "Donahue," and even "The Tonight Show" had changed the complexion of talk and information shows ten years later. These shows helped to create a new genre—information entertainment—that exploded on television in the 1980s.

People wonder how we compare to "Donahue." It comes down to discussing one subject versus variety. "Kelly & Company" delivers variety. We give the viewer music, humor, pathos, drama, and sensationalism all in one show.

One important ingredient, the glue in all of this, is the interviewer. Television audiences had gained a degree of sophistication about talk shows, talk show topics, and talk show hosts. My own standard for a good interviewer has always been to be direct, and to be confrontational only when necessary.

Whatever the approach, audiences identify with you as an interviewer. After all, you are asking the questions they would like to ask. The nature of those questions and the topics that are acceptable and unacceptable have changed dramatically in the world of information entertainment. On the 1972 edition of "Kelly & Company," we avoided some of the steamier topics of our times—topics that I felt at the time were too steamy for television, such as homosexuality or self-mutilation. But since that time, the subjects that were fit for television talk shows to explore changed enormously.

I knew that there was nothing in Rita's background or experience to prepare her for this kind of change in attitude. She was pure fifties local television, from her bouffant hairdo on the outside to the mind that functioned within. I had a "vision" at this point of how I wanted the show to go. I knew I wanted variety, and I knew I wanted a live audience. Even in the beginning we had people drifting into the studio, and I began playing to them.

We knew that with Rita the combination wasn't right. But there wasn't anything to do just then but get the show started with her and gather strength for our army.

THE CAMPAIGN FOR MARILYN TURNER

JOHN

I wasn't in on the planning of it, but in all honesty, I have to confess that I knew about it. The plans were to sneak Marilyn on the show for a guest appearance. It was a lousy thing to do to Rita, especially since the audience went wild, just exactly the way we figured they would. Marilyn didn't do very much during that conspiratorial debut. She just took a microphone and went through the audience, and they asked her some questions. It was more than enough to prove our point, that Marilyn was right for this sort of show. But Jeanne still would not let go of Rita.

However, she did try to provide a partial solution soon after that guest shot. Marilyn would be on the show on Tuesdays and Thursdays, and Rita would cohost on Mondays, Wednesdays, and Fridays. A few weeks more of this and Jeanne reversed herself, again by inches, with Marilyn doing Mondays, Wednesdays and Fridays, and Rita doing Tuesdays and Thursdays.

MARILYN

What a ridiculous way to do things! If you are going to do surgery, you use a sharp knife. Whoever heard of dragging two women on a string like that for months on end. It set everyone up for hard feelings.

I never fought to do the show the way John, Bob, and Hank Baskin did. They kept telling me that I could do it, but I never entirely believed that. I had never had any experience with anything like live interviews before. On TV I had always been formatted when I did the weather or when I was in acting situations where I had to learn lines.

Besides, I never thought I wanted to work that hard. The five-day-a-week weather seemed as big a steady commitment as I ever wanted to make. Plus, I had always been able to find other kinds of TV and advertising work when I wanted it.

Rita was rather cool toward me those last couple of months. I think she was hurt, partly judging from some snubs in the cafeteria. Interestingly enough, I always thought that the producers would have her back on the show in some way, and I think that the station had to pay her the balance of her contract when she finally left..

Bob Woodruff told me that the number of letters that the show received asking about her after she left was staggering. For a long while, people in the audience would ask about her too. As recently as last year, I saw a question in one of the columns of the local TV magazine asking what she is doing now.

By the time Rita left, the format of the program had been pretty well worked out, especially that one critical factor, the live audience. Bob Woodruff had produced a talk show in Philadelphia where he used a live audience, and he felt that it worked well. John has always loved it and found it an enormous stimulus. It took me a while to feel that same degree of comfort, though.

BOB WOODRUFF

I liked the idea that they were married. It was a novel thing in 1978. The weather girl thing had gone full cycle; they simply were no long accepted. I was fresh on the scene, and I wanted to revamp the show. John was hosting with a lady named Rita Bell, and he was still so conservative—that anchorman thing is hard to change. So I discussed it with Jeanne Findlater, and we worked it out. Marilyn was very refreshing. She was vivacious, inquisitive, asking the questions you really wanted to know. Even though she's a pretty blonde lady, people at home can identify with her—she always asks the questions you were afraid to ask. At the time, John had a tendency to be a little Ted Baxterish; he almost cupped his ear when he talked! But John's changed. Now he'll ask the real personal questions, and when I was still in Detroit, we'd give him the interviews where you wanted questions that might be embarrassing to Marilyn. But it was a while before I realized that John could be fun. We did a *Saturday Night Fever* show when that movie was so hot. Travolta's brother was on, and some dance instructor worked with John for about half an hour before the show, and he was great; they did a number together. No one in his wildest imagination would have thought he could do that.

Marilyn and John had their moments. They're both strong-minded people, and we'd joke for real that they sometimes were the Bickersons! Or she'd roar into my office and ask me to talk to that so-and-so, meaning John. And the same thing with him. It would drive him crazy when she'd run too long or be late for entrances or meetings or just about anything, because she's always late. But they were never, *never* "stars"—they did their jobs, only once in a while I'd have to talk to them like kids. There's a lot of tension in what they do, you know. Marilyn has a Marilyn Monroe quality. She's a very sexy lady, and I think she's as cute as a button. John always played the poor downtrodden husband. He's a very charming guy; what you see is what you get. He's really kind of quiet, but, strangely, he enjoys that studio audience. Yet he'd take off—and still does—for a Colorado horse ranch or some other godawful place.

Would I want to work with John and Marilyn again? Oh, of course. I love them dearly. They're just fun, even though we were fighting half the time. I think they're grateful for whatever I did. We ran Donahue right off the air. To this day, people of Multimedia say, "Oh, you're the one who destroyed us in Detroit!"

MARILYN

I had never done a lot of speaking in front of a live audience, and the thought of it scared me. I was protected by TV. Everything I had done previously meant learning lines and working in a studio.

There are other aspects of working with a live audience besides just looking out and seeing people looking back at you. One of these is using a hand microphone. In those early shows, I'd sometimes forget to take it with me when I would go out into the audience to take questions or I would find it awkward to use. John never had to struggle with that. He was used to sticking a microphone at people when he was a street reporter, but I had never done any interviews or on-the-spot reporting.

Today I can't imagine working without a live audience. Doing the weather all those years seems very confining when I look back on it now. You are given two or three minutes, and it is all formatted.

There are not many things that make me nervous now in regard to the show, and when something comes up that does, it usually has to do with subject matter rather than mechanics.

I always want to make sure I get every bit of information on the particular subject, particularly some of the medical topics like AIDS or SIDS. There might be a big introductory paragraph to present to the audience for background. Sometimes there might be videotape to accompany the segment or more than one guest to be interviewed for the same segment. In those situations, I find that I am concentrating on trying to keep everything straight—and that makes me nervous. Just try to keep clear on some of the sex things that we get into on the show, like transvestite transsexuals who were married to homosexuals and have ten kids! I can get so wound up with that. I mean, there you are on the air and you have to keep it all straight.

Sometimes in the middle of it all, I'll start thinking, "Wait a minute! Would he want to do *that* with *him* if *he* was actually thinking that *he* was a *she?*"

We deal with those things on the show, but I really wonder how many of these people are, deep down inside, laughing up their sleeves at us.

JEANNE FINDLATER

In the early days of the show, I remember we had a lot of conversations about what to do and how to do certain things. Once a month the producers would get together for a couple of hours and brainstorm. We were hunting, changing certain things, and regrouping to create the right "on-the-air" personality for John and Marilyn as a couple. Maybe they would have come up with some of these approaches on their own, but often in television, you don't have all the time in the world to experiment or to hunt and peck. As it was, we were fortunate that we did have a couple of years before we had any local competition from the "Sonya" show, and by then we were beating out "Donahue" in popularity in the local ratings.

We told them particularly that it was all right to express a certain intimacy on the air. They *are* husband and wife, not strangers. So why should you act like strangers on the air? It's all right to be somewhat personal; there are certain little things that husbands and wives know about one another or share that are titillating to other people.

For example, John might say something to the effect of—"I can always tell when Marilyn's mad. She finishes a sentence!"

But by the same token, you can't step over the line of being too personal. You can't go that next step and tell the audience too much about yourself. And they never, ever have. Their instincts about this are uncannily good. They know exactly how far to go,

136

but at the same time they are willing to go right to the limit, right to the edge of that point.

I think the reason they can walk this fine line is that they are so comfortable together, both in their roles as married partners and as professional partners. They have made many references to their marital relationship, talking things through or arguing constructively or kissing and making up. I think that these things are pleasant identification and serve a positive purpose for the audience.

Marilyn particularly can get quite personal and even outrageous on the air if the subject suggests itself. I don't think we ever had to coax this kind of material out of her, but rather applauded it when it presented itself. I am a great believer in rewarding the right behaviors rather than coming down on a person for negative ones.

Yet, there were other things that we had to take cognizance of that are part of their personalities. Early on, we tried having them both in the kitchen for cooking segments, each puttering and interviewing the chef. It was a disaster. They were mugging and upstaging one another without let-up. It didn't seem to go over on live TV. It seemed that the best approach was to have them function separately but equally by dividing up the interviews.

For John, the hardest part of the new show was accepting that it wasn't hard—that he was doing a talk show situation just right and that he shouldn't mind that he liked it so much.

It is much different being a journalist doing an interview "out in the field" than it is doing an interview on a talk show like "Kelly & Company." As a journalist, you ask questions, you get your answers, and you try not to put yourself into the result. You are a conduit for information. An interview on "Kelly & Company" is different, for you can and *should* bring some of your*self* into it.

Everybody who has come from doing the news to a talk show situation struggles to some degree with this attitude. They seem to have this big "J" burned into their flesh. We had a lot of conversations about this, and John needed a lot of convincing that he hadn't lost his newsman's reputation and sacrificed something by doing this.

I think that this struggle kept him wedded to the one evening news show at six for two years, even though it was a very long day in combination with "Kelly & Company" at nine in the morning. He was getting increasingly irritable and tense from feeling himself pulled in two directions. One night when I was in his office he exploded, "For two cents I'd take this whole damn job and shove it."

I told him that I would give him the two cents. Again, he worried. What if the morning show should get canceled or scrapped? Then he would be destroyed from ever going back to news.

I assured him that, not only would he be able to go back to news if that should happen, but that I envisioned that his role as a talk show host would broaden. John loves to say that I take credit for all of the success of "Kelly & Company," that I have been quoted in the newspapers and all. But wasn't I right about all of it?

MARILYN

As partners in work as well as in marriage, John and I are merged together in many more ways than most married couples. There are a few things that we do to give ourselves some space. We both drive our own

JOHN

Me with my mother and father, Port Charlotte, Florida, just a couple of years ago.

I'm launching a hot air balloon with the great "Meeeechigan" play-by-play man, Bob Ufer.

Scuba diving is one of my favorite hobbies. My buddy Jim Gross and I were checking out our new gear in the pool—hot dog divers!

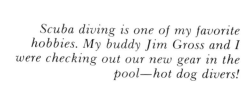

I just love to ride. Here I am in the Colorado Rockies aboard Glory.

MARILYN
Here I am with Dad and Mom.

I'm a proud mother with my two sons. How did they get so big?

Here I am with Twilight, a member of our very large family of pets.

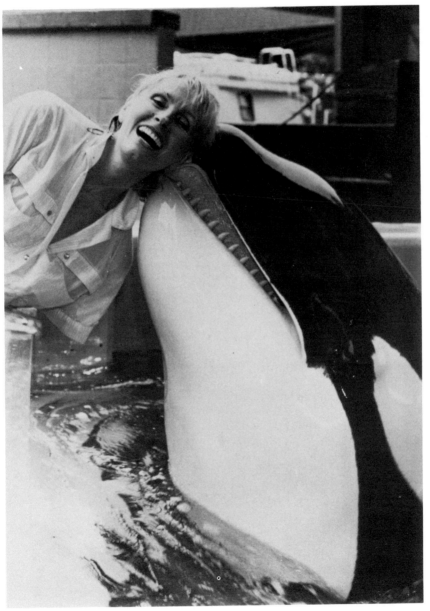

I'm being kissed by Shamu, the amorous killer whale, at Sea World, Ohio.

Dean escorted me to a downtown function John chose to skip.

Cross-country skiing with Pashtu, another of our brood.

We're both very involved in animal rights. Here we are with friend David Wills, Executive Director of the Michigan Humane Society, and Nigel, a starving lion cub that David was nursing back to health.

On the grounds of Tara, our dream home in West Bloomfield, with Billy showing us the way.

Coming down the aisle December 27, 1974. Behind us are Sylvia Straith, Marilyn's matron of honor and best friend, and my best man, Bill Combe.

Here we are at the wedding party with a modestly dressed Bob Talbert.

On our new boat, the Co-Host.

We've made it through a few administrations. Here we are with President Gerald Ford.

And here's Marilyn with President Ronald Reagan.

Nice guy John Forsythe with Marilyn and the 1983 staff of "Kelly & Company."

A little glamour—celebrating the first anniversary of "Good Afternoon Detroit" at the Roostertail.

Rehearsing with Tristan Rogers (Scorpio) and Emma Samms for a guest role on "General Hospital," 1985.

For once, my plan backfired and Soupy Sales laid one on me.

Marilyn having fun with a couple of professional wrestlers.

Marilyn working out with a long-haired Arnold Schwarzenegger.

The immortal Red Skelton, our favorite guest. Photo by Charles D. Derry

Chatting with Paul Williams. Photo by Charles D. Derry

Chuck Norris debating with the audience. Should he belt me with the bottle?   Photo by Charles D. Derry

The very talented Ben Vereen.   Photo by Charles D. Derry

Shari Lewis and Lamb Chop. Photo by Charles D. Derry

Marilyn cradles a newborn baby girl delivered by cesarean section on the air on "Kelly & Company"—a first.

cars to and from work. We never go to the studio together.

Several years ago we decided too much togetherness can make a dull marriage. So at least once, maybe twice, a year we do what *we want* to do. John goes off with his close friend David Wills to ride in Colorado or Arizona, and I usually pack up my mom and we head for Ft. Meyers, Florida, to visit my oldest son, Rob, and his wife, Judy, and my two "grandchildren," Garbo and Domino. They're dobermans—no *real* grandchildren yet.

DAVID WILLS

I'm the Executive Director of the Michigan Humane Society, and I met Marilyn before John. She was the animal person, and we dealt with humaneness. I didn't meet John for some time, until she said we've got to have dinner. Then I discovered that he liked the South and its history, and I like the South and its history. He likes horses, I like horses. A lot of other common interests—he'd flown planes years ago, and I fly. He likes racing race cars and driving them; so do I. And suddenly it was a checklist of things we liked. It was 1983, and finally he opened up and took me riding. I right then bought a horse and stabled it with him, and we've spent a lot of time together. There's a side of John others don't see. I see the masculine, adventuresome John. Now he's the consummate suburbanite, a cosmopolitan man. But I've seen him stand on the high sides of the Colorado mountains with a slicker on, pipe in his mouth, and the rain coming down. I think he was born a couple hundred years too late because John Kelly would have liked to have broken open the country, to see it with his horse. This isn't hype; he can do it. He knows how to cross, rides great, can make his fires and his bedroll—John really gets into it. This past June he took over from a wrangler-guide who was flat lost, and John got us down and out. Rain and all. And John looks the part—I think he sometimes feels like he was there.

I also believe because he's a gentleman he runs the risk of people trying to take advantage of him. But those with the impression that he can be walked over are wrong. Inside there's a really bright mind that doesn't go anywhere he doesn't want to go. Now, he's in a business that is anything but gentle, but I think he's come a long way without changing one of his principles, and there aren't many who can say that. The John Kelly I know could have gone further with his career, probably, but at what price? He's consistent. For instance, his friendship. A few years ago I got into trouble when it was revealed that I had lied about part of my resumé, my credentials. The news media in this town had a field day. Channel Four really nailed me, even had fun with me. John and Marilyn took me out to dinner the same night, and it was like a personal mark: "He's our friend." I remember him saying, "Number one, no one is perfect, and number two, it's none of their damned business." I know a lot of media people in this town, and only with John and Marilyn was it friendship first, the hell with the story. John and I have become very close friends.

It must be hard to be John Kelly and Marilyn Turner. John's strength and honesty—hell, the classic word is *gentleman*. He's a throwback to a time when culture, manners, and charm had a much higher value than today. But when John feels he's been wronged, he'll turn quickly. Columnists have written, when John and Marilyn took separate vacations (he and I off to the mountains and the horses), that they were getting a divorce. That really hurt. He got bent out of shape and won't talk to those people—any of them—to this day. I've told him that's a weakness, but it eats him up. They love each other, you know.

I like the way he's still nice to Marilyn; he still buys her little things. And do they work for the Michigan Humane Society! They've come in for a nighttime benefit when they had to get up at 4:30 the next morning. And they give a lot of money to the society. Once when John and I were out west, there were poor kids working at the ranch. One boy was trying to learn guitar, but he didn't have one. Well, it turns out it was his birthday, and John said, "Hey, let's buy him a guitar." And we did—never saw him again after that.

I guess you get the idea I like John Kelly and Marilyn Turner. Damned right. But John and I are close. I think I know him. Nothing's going to make him ready for the rocking chair. He's got a list of things he's going to accomplish. He does so many things well.

MARILYN

I think the question of how we can work together and live together day-in, day-out, is our *most* frequently asked question from our studio audience. It can be a pain. You do have to create space for yourself and we have worked it out. I notice that when we come home after work, we don't talk to each other for about an hour or so. He does his thing and I do mine. It's a pattern that has developed over the years and it works well. I must admit that there

141

have been times when I could barely stand to look at John. I have gotten so angry that I could not stand the sight of him, but I can always perform.

Sometimes I think that we're two people doing the work of four people, especially when we were hosting the afternoon show in addition to "Kelly & Company," but the fact that we are husband and wife helps a lot. We can ad-lib, even for a whole segment if need be, and our conversation just sort of flows. The audience may think a lot of the stuff we do is scripted, but ninety-five percent of it is spontaneous and ad-libbed. A husband and wife have that frame of reference to build upon, and some funny things have come out. In fact, I am amazed at the funny things that do come out. We have compared the way I keep the top of my dresser to the way John keeps his, and we've discussed John's vasectomy.

When I'm asked how many kids we have, I say five, but we didn't make *any* together. John says, "Marilyn had me 'fixed' before we got married," which is true! I usually say I had him "spayed" or "neutered," which always brings down the house as everyone in Detroit knows of our great dedication to the Michigan Humane Society and its spay and neuter campaign to lower the number of dogs and cats that are born without consideration for overpopulation.

Also, I'm always catching John on sexist things. One morning John was telling the audience—"Oh sure, that's how all men feel." Well, you look at the men in the audience and you *know* they are all going to agree with him. I'll take a shot at that, and he'll do one of his poor, dumb guy double takes. Then I'll take another shot, and it gets to be funny.

One bit we did recently in closing a show and

saying good-bye came right after a cooking segment.

JOHN

Oh, my God. Was that gross. Out of nowhere, just as if we were sitting at home, Marilyn leans over to me and says—"I've been eating onions. Do I smell bad?" And with that, she breathes right in my face.

I said, "No," and fainted right off my chair. Now you know you wouldn't do that unless it was your husband—or your wife.

The audience's response to something like this helps enormously. The audience—God love 'em—bails us out a lot of the time. Especially with ticklish subjects. Do women have more affairs than men? Do you remember your first affair? What did you do on your wedding night? Marilyn loves to ask those kinds of questions. She'll go right out there, holding the microphone, and all of a sudden they'll look at her and talk. And you can't believe what they're talking about—for example, hemorrhoids.

MARILYN

I'm not embarrassed talking about it. Our *dear* friend and former producer, Dan Weaver, now production coordinator for the soap, "Capitol," always shared this human misery and, probably because of this, we did a segment on the subject for "Kelly & Company." We probably were the first to do this in the country.

DAN WEAVER

I was with the show for four years, two as an

143

associate producer, then I left and was with Donahue for four months before I was offered the spot of senior producer for Kelly. I grabbed it and stayed for two years before leaving to join the staff of "Capitol" here in Los Angeles. Nancy Lenzen brought me to Detroit from Cleveland, where I had known her on the "Morning Exchange." I missed meeting Marilyn when I was there for my interview but did spend a lot of time with John. That morning they'd done a show that didn't work, and he was honest about it, and that made me feel good. It was nice. And that honesty continued. I mean John was almost father to that show, and when we started getting overnights (ratings), there were times when we producers took them too literally. He'd say, "Do the best show you can and don't look at overnights; look at the month's worth." He really did have a lot of experience; he was more mature. I've worked on shows where ratings were a problem, and there was a great deal of tension, like now on "Capitol." But John and Marilyn have loyalties and people who are loyal to them. Bob Woodruff once called them "Sonny and Cher of Detroit," but they're more than that. People know they can trust them.

I always thought Marilyn was terribly refreshing. At first she's someone you have to watch. I didn't care for her when I arrived on the scene, but the first respect came when I saw her love for animals. Once they were out of town, and I decided to do a fur fashion show. Somehow she learned about it and called me, and after talking it over, she said, "Do it if you think you should." But she convinced me, and I killed the segment. We've never done furs on "Kelly & Company." She and John are against it, but Marilyn started it all. There's this comedian, Rip Taylor, who came roaring on the show wearing a fur coat. At one point he said to her, "Here, try this on; eat your heart out." Right there, on camera, live, Marilyn said, "No, I don't believe in killing animals." He was *pissed off*, but to her, it was important not to have any part of that.

Father Andrew Greeley, always frank about celibacy and all, was with us once. I had given Marilyn a question about priests and masturbation. Looking over the questions before the show, she almost died, and I said, "Well, play it by ear." She didn't do it. I was standing behind the cameras near the end of the interview. I wanted her to do it, so I made a little masturbatory gesture, and she almost fell apart and didn't ask. She was probably right.

There were times when Marilyn bugged me, though. So very good when she was on—always late. I got so tired of dragging her into the studio, I decided to teach her a lesson. She missed our opening announcement—she came flying into the studio as John was doing the thing alone. I turned to her and said, "You weren't here; we're doing it without you." She was OK for a couple of weeks, and then it was back to the same way. One of us would go get her and lead her in by the hand. Just not conscious of time. I suppose we producers sort of acted like parents who want their kids to do well. We helped too much.

I had a lot of respect for John and all of his experience. He'd done it all—or had it done to him. Still, there were times when he was leery of some of the things we tried to do. Our informal motto was "young, fun, and number one." It meant a creative environment, but working with someone experienced was really great—and he was. Marilyn would do pretty much what we wanted, but John would back off sometimes. He was the balance. The longer

I'm away from it, the more I realize what a good working relationship there was.

There was a lot of practical joking. One day we were doing something on funerals, and we had a coffin there to use as part of the discussion on costs. So I hid in it, and when Marilyn walked by I leaped out and cried, "Good morning!" Well, she almost died. That was always going on. One morning, the day of a very important show, John privately told everyone on the staff—I mean everyone—to call in sick. I took the calls one after the other. I was close to being committed before they all walked in together, laughing. There were many things like that, and all of them tension reducers. Sometimes we needed that badly. John and Marilyn felt it, too— maybe more than others. There were times when they would spat in the office. Once in a while it may have been evident on the air. When it happened, I think people knew it. And because producers are sometimes schemers, I think I liked that.

Celebrities on occasion could get to them. Henny Youngman once out-onelined John. Finally, John looked at him and said, "I'm in awe," and Henny replied, "Well, get out of there." And then the show on which we placed a secret call to President Carter, so that Rosalyn, our guest, could talk with him. All very fine, but the phone line was bad, and they couldn't hear each other. And there John sat, trying to stay calm.

Helen Reddy, with Marilyn. I think she was going through something painful in her personal life, and all she gave Marilyn were two-word answers. Finally, Marilyn gently said something about Ms. Reddy being uncomfortable, and "It's best if we end the interview now." Marilyn was really upset afterward, thinking maybe there was something she could have done.

They were always cooperative, but Marilyn was gutsier than John sometimes, probably because she trusted us so much, she'd do just about anything. John wanted to, but a few times something would stop him short. At Sea World we had a great opening. John's part was to come riding into the beach running a small, really tiny powerboat. At the last minute, he said it wasn't safe, so they came in on another boat, and it just wasn't the same. Later we found out that, unknown to us, there were sandbags hidden in the boat John refused to use and which we didn't know about, and when John added power during practice it almost went over backward. It was too late to do anything about it then.

I'll always remember a letter we got from a woman who had watched a program on SIDS, Sudden Infant Death Syndrome. Marilyn had done a wonderful, tender, and understanding job. The writer said she enjoyed it, little suspecting it would soon happen to her. When her baby died, she said she remembered what she'd learned from "Kelly & Company" and thought she could make it through.

MARILYN

I guess what we are really saying is that audiences are wonderful; they are the backbone of our show. Oftentimes, with guests, they'll be the ones who will pop the nastiest or most controversial questions that everyone is dying to know. But you have to prime them, spend time with them. Otherwise, you will get a dead audience at 9:00 A.M. because they are not used to the studio, the technicians, the lights, and the cameras. You've got to get them thinking. They don't think of themselves as part of the show until you tell them they are part of the show. John does that, the warm-up ten minutes before the show. Before John comes out, usually about fifteen minutes before we go on the air, one of our producers, Jill Coughlin, does the warm-up for the warm-up.

JOHN

One morning right after we started having a live audience, I said, "Let's have a warm-up just like the network guys do!" Carson, Donahue, they all have them. Donahue does his own. Carol Burnett made her warm-up part of her show when she was on nighttime TV, but she did a warm-up before the warm-up.

I have some basic material that I use. Marilyn thinks it's corny, but I know it will never fail to get a laugh. For example, I'll count from one through ten asking the women in the audience how many children they have. I'll raise my voice, and my eyebrows, as I get into the higher numbers, but it is the laughers and the reacters that I am really looking for. I am looking at them while they are looking at me. We're checking each other out.

MIKE DUFFY

I have been the *Free Press* TV critic since 1980. I guess you could deduce that I watch a lot of television. Too much.

During a ratings sweep month I get very cynical about how the game operates, because it can be a very cynical game. My standards are strict, and I've admitted up front that I am a fuddy-duddy traditionalist about how news ought to be played on TV. I think local TV news tends to blur the line between what is news and what is show business.

A show like "Kelly & Company" is a different thing. It passes out information, but its intention is to entertain. You have fashion, you have celebrities, cooks dropping by, a certain amount of glitz. And I think that it is one of the most successful local productions of its type in the country in combining these elements.

What I have to watch out for as a TV critic is that the show is not made for me. It is not aimed at a male audience. There are not that many males around watching TV at nine in the morning. The average viewer of a morning talk show is more than likely going to be a female, maybe with a few kids, who will be watching TV while doing something else or in short bursts. Maybe the average viewer will be between household chores, or running in and out of the room, or reading a newspaper or book. Those in charge at "Kelly & Company" use market research, like any other TV production, to determine what components they will use and how well they use the mix.

The big trick to success on television is being able to make it personal. TV critics like to bash news anchors, for example, for being just readers. But there is a talent there, a facility for being able to come into people's homes and have them *want* to watch you and feel comfortable with you. John and Marilyn both come off extremely well on camera. He is glib and good-looking, and she is blonde and pretty. They have that ability to be there on camera and have people feel, "Oh, these are our friends."

I've been on TV in interview situations a number of times, and it can be pretty intimidating. You are enclosed in a studio, and even with all of these technical people running around, you feel like you are in a vacuum. It's no small accomplishment to break through that, make it all sound natural, and say—"Hi, everybody. Here's what's happening in Detroit." The live audience helps John and Marilyn out of this void, and that's an important part of the chemistry. They work the studio audience well.

But a key part to the chemistry of the show is the husband-wife thing, and there hasn't really been any other local show able to compete with that.

I think that the "Sonya" show was ultimately hurt by their popularity. John and Marilyn had been on a couple of years by the time she got her show started, and it took them that long to get their show down to a smooth well-running hum. But Sonya came at them with a very slick, well-produced show. Post Newsweek was her syndicator, and they don't mess around. But there was a little too much "touchy-feely" seventies mentality going on. She'd get too heavy into doom-gloom topical stuff. But, ultimately, I think it boiled down to the fact that people in this market want to see John and Marilyn.

What is more, *sex sells*. I have also observed that newspapers are not immune to this phenomenon. We sell more papers on Mondays when we run the topless bar ads. There is real interest in the two of them as a couple; when they were married, when they weren't, when they got married to each other. I always get letters about them; some are catty, and some are positive, but I am always amazed at the amount of personal involvement that the viewers take. And this is aside from the subject matter that they will deal with, the trashiest, most provocative stuff that all of these shows—including the nightly news—load up the schedules with during the ratings periods in November, February, and May.

But the show is a success for many reasons, and the producers are a key part of it. Nancy Lenzen, who worked with Bob Woodruff and then took over when he left Detroit, heads a very sharp staff. Without that kind of professional behind-the-scenes help, that show would not be what it is.

9
JUST TO PROVE
THAT WE'RE L·I·V·E

MARILYN

We're in our ninth year with the show. With that many shows, it's hard to pick out the high points. Every couple of days something will stand out that you'll think was really working well.

Another element that works differently in the world of TV is time. Time moves so quickly on the show that we don't have a chance to think about which were "the best" shows. I'll know who is on for tomorrow, but I barely remember who was on yesterday. All of us do our jobs, and we don't really have time to sit down and think.

We work in different ways. There are certain things that will click for me that may not work as well for John, and vice versa. For example, I like the "soap" stars very much. I think that they are pretty intelligent and usually a lot of fun. They are not too full of themselves, and I am always surprised at the degree of involvement the audience feels for their roles. We usually do "questions" from the audience when we have the soap people on, mainly because there is so much interest. The audience will ask them questions by the name of the characters they play and always want to know what is coming up next in the plots.

Probably the most beautiful woman we have ever had on the show is the actress Jaclyn Smith. She came on wearing virtually no makeup at nine in the morning and was absolutely gorgeous. I had interviewed her two years before when she had just finished playing Jackie Kennedy in the made-for-TV movie. I got a great insight into how a truly beautiful woman perceives herself. When I told her that she was exceptionally beautiful, it didn't shock her exactly but she immediately zeroed in on the flaws. "You know, I hate my legs, and if you'll notice, I have a large zit on my cheek today that I had *some time* covering." As a matter of fact, she thinks Cheryl Ladd is gorgeous and has always felt when they were doing "Charlie's Angels" that Farrah and Cheryl were much prettier than she. It's amazing what we see when we look in the mirror.

We've had Barbara Walters on twice. She's very tough, and you cannot trick her. John was interviewing her at her last appearance, and she was very insistent about whether the woman cohost on the show got to do the heavy-duty interviews. She wanted to know why I wasn't doing her interview. We explained that I had interviewed David Hartman the previous day, and we tried to divide things evenly.

During the Republican convention of 1980 in Detroit, we had Nancy Reagan as a guest. We met briefly for a chat before we went on the air. That is not typical procedure for the show unless the guest has enormous visibility and clout, which, of course, Nancy Reagan does. Usually we do not see the guests until we go on the air. Somewhere in the course of chatting with her, I told her I was born in Canada, and still maintain my citizenship in that country. Her reply was—"You mean you won't be able to vote for my husband?" I thought I might have thrown the whole interview into jeopardy.

I found her very close-mouthed, very, very cautious and guarded. But I kept going with it, probing until I could find a subject that she felt comfortable with. She finally softened up a bit when she started talking about her son's Little League baseball games and about when her husband was governor and the family lived in Sacramento.

There are a few authors that I have great fun with. Judith Krantz is one; she is funny, lively, and very down to earth. A good interview. With a super author like her, we ask personal questions, not about the book. We de-plug the book.

The reason we don't see guests before is that *we* as the interviewers don't want the interview done in the waiting room (we call it the "green room" and, naturally, it's *not green!*). It wouldn't be fresh. Also, if you get into conversation, you may get, "I'd rather not discuss that" or "I don't want to talk about my ex-husband," or whatever. This makes for a very dull on-air interview and is a definite no-no. I ran into Priscilla Presley in the bathroom (even "celebrities" have that little preshow trip), and she began to tell me she *didn't/wouldn't* talk about Elvis Presley. I got around that by asking about her daughter's musical ability and she forgot her request and discussed similarities between her daughter and Elvis. I got lucky, but see what I mean?

I consider my job as being "on the air," and I don't think about anything else. John, on the other hand, is constantly worrying about what to me are silly matters such as camera angles, lighting arrangements, and the appearance of the set.

I must love this business. As I said before, I thought twice about doing this show, because I had never worked this hard and this many hours before. But it is not performing that wears you down. It is all of the other petty things.

Most women would think having their makeup and hair done twice a day (we did "Good Afternoon Detroit" for four years along with "Kelly & Company") would be *wonderful!* Well it's great to have very talented people doing it, and we have them. Sandra Moyer and Robin Monoogian are definitely not only the best makeup people in Detroit but in any other major city. As a matter of fact, I've learned so much from them that I went on to do some research and have launched my own skin care products called The Difference. It's *got* to be more successful than the dress shop, because I know more about this than I did about the rag business!

Janice Phillips is a *fabulous* hairdresser. I've gotten to the point that I *never* worry what I look like—I have complete faith and trust in my staff's talent and ability and that's the *best* compliment I can give them. They care and they're great. Jacqueline Bisset was asked if she didn't worry about looking good all the time. Her reply was, "My job is acting and doing the very best I can for a part—I have great people doing my hair and makeup. I rarely look at myself before going in to shoot." Boy, is that true.

However, sitting still all that time can be trying. Getting my clothes together—with the two shows I changed twice a day—means I have to have everything at my fingertips—stockings, accessories, scarves, belts, jewelry, shoes, etc. In most cases, you end up putting it together in a *big hurry*. My aforementioned hair and makeup people coordinated everything beautifully. Of course my whole wardrobe "lives" in my office.

When Friday night comes, I have to pack a bag to go home for the weekend. I go back and forth every day in cotton jumpsuits for summer and wool for winter, the "mainstay" of my "at-home" wardrobe.

I have an arrangement for my clothes. The station has a "trade" deal for clothes for me with Roz and Shern, an elegant women's store. They give the store credits on the show and I get to keep the clothes. The dollar figure is set up at the beginning of the year and a contract signed for the trade-out.

Other things that go along with the job are production meetings before and after the show. The mail is endless (of course, it's welcome because that means they like us out there). Telephone calls to viewers and keeping track of our appearances are other important parts of the show. Thanks to the "Kelly & Company" secretary, Dani Jacobson, those important parts are taken care of; we would be at a loss without her.

JOHN

On occasion it's apparent to viewers that all is not as advertised on "Kelly & Company," simply because a promised guest doesn't show up. Many times the fault lies with a delayed flight, illness, or an error in scheduling. There have been times when our staff has chosen *not* to present someone who is already in our green room. In those cases, it's perhaps an attitude problem, refusal to carry out a promise for which we have prepared, and other things.

There are also the times when the "Kelly & Company" staff has practiced a teeny weeny deception. Some years ago Christina Crawford, daughter of the late Joan Crawford, was in town briefly plugging the controversial book, *Mommy Dearest*, in which daughter did not treat mother kindly. Despite our best efforts, commitments on the part of Ms. Crawford's publicist made it impossible for her to appear on our show. In fact, her only appearance in town was on a Channel Four weekly show called "Studio D," which is no longer on the air. We finally gave up. Two days later, at about a quarter past eight, the guard at the gate called to inform us a limo was there containing Ms. Crawford. "Send her right up," producer Nancy Lenzen said without hesitation, and hurried to meet her and escort her to an empty studio temporarily in use as a green room. Nancy was smooth. To all appearances, Ms. Crawford was not only expected, but was our featured guest for the day.

Meanwhile, in the office, the staff was frantically reshuffling the program; reducing time allotted to others to make room for Crawford. Back in the green room, Ms. Crawford was unaware she was at the wrong television station, but was gazing with puzzlement at her printed schedule, which outlined her city-to-city appearances.

"You know, my dear." she said to Nancy, "I just don't see anything here about a 'Kelly & Company,' just 'Studio D.' "

Nancy didn't turn a hair. "Oh, 'Studio D' refers to

this room, our temporary green room. It's really a studio."

Crawford nodded. A crisis had passed. Later she went on the air, and it was a success.

Years later, the Channel Four producer changed jobs and is now on the staff at our station. Nancy recently made a joke about the Christina Crawford incident of days gone by, but the producer was not amused.

As "Kelly & Company" guests, animals sometimes cooperate, sometimes they don't. They just don't seem to really care about red lights on cameras and floor managers' frantic signals. There was the bear that wrestled a dwarf (one of our classier presentations) and afterward drank a Coke and did what my mother called Number One *and* Number Two on Detroit's "Only Live Morning Talk Show."

Another fun time was when we originated the entire show via satellite from Sea World of Ohio. Thousands of people from the Detroit area had made the trip to the Cleveland area, and the weather was wonderful. Our planned opening segment on the second of two days there was with the killer whales led by Shamu. They were wonderful, performing great arching leaps from the water, going through hoops and over hurdles. The audiences loved them. That was in rehearsal. Then, the moment for live television came. The opening of the show. With great fanfare and thunderous applause, Marilyn and I appeared, welcomed one and all. We introduced Shamu and his friends. Great dramatic music . . . fountains spraying . . . a wide shot of the whale pool.

No whales.

Oh, they were there all right, they just didn't feel

like jumping out of the water anymore. So they didn't. We hemmed and hawed. The trainers hemmed and hawed, with a dash of embarrassment. Nothing worked. We learned later that they were suspicious of us. We had mounted a platform just above the pool for the opening, and they saw us, knew things were not as they should be, and decided to play it safe.

And just like animals, there are some terrific people and some not so terrific. But the humans should know better. Take the story of three musicians, a study in contrasts. These three gentlemen stand out from many who have been with us. Ronnie Millsap, a country and western singer, composer, performer. In booking his appearance, publicists assured us he would sing and play prior to his interview. We scheduled him to open the show. The appointed day arrived and so did he. But he refused to sing, refused to play, and was impolite to our staff. Our producer at the time, Dan Weaver, went to talk to him. Returning to the office, Dan grimly informed us he invited Mr. Millsap to leave. Which he did. In a rage.

Another pianist-singer-performer we had on the show was Bobby Short. He was big in New York and in what used to be called café society. Once again, we were assured he would play. Our stage people built a small set to resemble a nightclub. The segment opened with me standing next to Bobby, who was seated at a baby grand. A bit of conversation and then I asked him to play. Bobby Short looked up at me and said flatly, "Bobby Short does not play in the morning." I ended the segment immediately.

Then there was another pianist, Peter Duchin. He was a complete gentleman and a delightful interview. Appearing two days after the death of Alan J.

160

Lerner, Peter, without notice, played a marvelous medley of Lerner music from many Broadway hit shows, then crossed to sit with me and discussed his father (the great thirties and forties bandleader Eddy Duchin), his home with Averell Harriman, his bands, the Kennedys, the Maria Shriver–Arnold Schwarzenegger wedding—all with the panache of a born storyteller and humorist. Afterward he thanked the audience and the stagehands, assured us he would be back, and departed. A dream guest.

Another memorable guest was Imogene Coca. A few years ago she was playing at the Fisher Theatre in Detroit. Naturally, we wanted her as a guest and she agreed to appear. The night before, she fell off the stage and was bruised, sprained, strained, and battered. We learned this only when we spotted this hunched and limping small person creeping down the hall toward our offices at half past seven the following day. Her voice was querulous and faint, sentences trailing off as she looked at our producer, misty-eyed. She was helped into the green room and given tea as the producer rushed into our offices. The woman is ill; she's hurt. Should we go on? Yes, she said she could and an enormous crowd (for us) had gathered to see her. Back to the green room went our producer. It was suggested someone would help her on to the set and to her chair. No, she thought she could probably make it on her own. Our producer fled again, afraid to tire her further with questions. By now we were all in near panic but felt it was too late to do anything else without risking insulting this fine comedienne.

The appointed hour arrived, as it always does. I, with fear and concern concealed, introduced the great Imogene Coca. She veritably leaped into the studio, eyes sparkling, cheeks flushed, and with an enormous smile. The interview was filled with stories and laughs, stories and pathos. She had the audience and me in the palm of her hand. At the end, she waved, smiled, and strode out of the studio with the vigor of a twenty-one-year-old Olympic runner. It was a wonderful performance. And it was a performance.

Later, I was told, she immediately began to limp and shuffle. But when the lights were on and with the sound of the applause, she became a professional. Hats off and a deep bow to Imogene Coca.

This is in stark contrast to actress Elizabeth Ashley who showed up late and only after a telephone call from our office, complaining of a bad cold, a late night, Michigan weather, and Detroit people. She was there to plug a book but acted as if it were against her will. Her language was beyond vulgar, her behavior inexcusable. At one point, her escort was nasty enough to arouse the anger of producer Randy Barrone, and for a while it looked like fist city.

Another scuffle, this time with Tony Danza, was averted through the intervention of one of our cameramen. Once again, it was one of those situations where Tony's publicist had agreed to a small skit involving him with the hosts without, apparently, telling his client. Danza arrived in a foul mood and didn't want to do a sketch, didn't want to do much of anything, and was quite rude. It was then that help arrived in the person of studio cameraman Jerry Zuckerman. Somehow, he took Danza aside and said something like, "I'm from Brooklyn—you're from Brooklyn," the trouble disappeared, and he was an excellent guest. Later we learned that Danza had been going through a particularly trying period in his personal and professional life, and it had just gotten to him.

As for the award for the prince of the nice people, it's a draw between Red Skelton and Richard Simmons. We'll always remember Red. A gentle man, a wonderful performer and artist. For thirty minutes he held the audience in the palm of his hand. He did all of the wonderful routines for which he is famous, including working with the old felt hat . . . ad-libbing with audience members, answering their questions with candor and honesty. Afterward, he climbed the steps to our second floor control room to meet our director, Mason Weaver, a gesture that made Mason's decade.

To top it off, later in the show, I was doing a bit with a local lady who is a professional witch. Gundella the witch. (It was near Halloween.) Once again, we had a set that denoted the aspect of the day—spooky lights, weird music. At one point Gun-della was explaining how she cast a spell when, completely unexpected, Red walked in with a small bundle of firewood, laid it at Gundella's feet, and tried to light it. I was wiped out, the audience was on the floor, and Gundella was hysterical. One of the great moments and, of course, the tape has disap-peared. I will never forget the great Red Skelton.

Our other favorite is Richard Simmons. Can enough be said about Richard? He is a sweet man with great loyalties. They extend to "Kelly & Com-pany" for a couple of reasons, not the least of which is this was his first talk show, and one on which we allow Richard to do what he wants because we believe in him and trust him. Once, on the air, the outrageous Richard said that with his body and her legs he and Marilyn must have a baby!

But the best of Richard is the time we had an important location show scheduled from a local mall. Thousands turned out. Our special guest was to have been Minnie Pearl. Three days before the show, Minnie was forced to cancel because of illness which eventually led to surgery. She's fine now and I'm glad of it, but at the time we were desperate. We cast about for a star until the next day when, once again, we imposed on Richard. Nancy called Los Angeles and encountered one of Richard's people who explained it was impossible, that he was much too busy, and that it simply couldn't be done. Nancy patiently explained that she would just like to talk to Richard. Minutes later he was on the phone and said quietly, "I'll be there." And he was, and he was dynamite. That's the kind of guy he is. Don't ever knock Richard Simmons in our presence. Ever.

Cooks are always fun, but you never know if they're going to finish on time or how it's going to turn out. My two favorite memories concern Julia Child and local chef Maria Ang. Julia prepared an omelet, then zapped it with a propane torch and burned it to a crisp. Calmly, with that distinctive voice, she remarked, "Mr. Kelly, I have burned the omelet." What could I do? I ate it.

But Maria gets the high goof award for one of her many appearances. She was preparing a wok dish and tossed in, I think, cayenne peppercorns. The studio filled with acrid blue smoke and fumes. Throats closed, eyes watered, and people gagged. The entire audience began to choke and cough, as did I. Maria tried to tough it out, but I surrendered and called for a commercial break. We kicked open the doors and let the exhaust fans do the rest. Funny thing, I was the only one who tried the dish. I can't recall what it was . . . but it was good!

10
WHAT IS IT EXACTLY
THAT YOU DO—ANYWAY?

THOM SHARPE

I'm more nervous before "Kelly & Company" than any other talk show that I do, even though I have done it at least twenty-five times and I've been on three times as substitute host. I have forgotten whole verses of songs that I've been singing. I've even seen my entire life come flashing before my eyes as if in one glorious blaze before the inferno.

What's the big deal about "Kelly & Company"? Well, first off, it's home. I grew up in West Dearborn, and when I come in to do the show, I always stay at the Hotel Mom. I figure that there will be a few people coming to the studio from the old neighborhood. That always sends the adrenaline pumping.

Second, a live studio audience is a scary thing for a comedian to contemplate. Sometimes, in taping a TV show with an audience, the producers will go back and add a laugh if something doesn't work. That's called "sweetening" in the comedy business. But a morning show with a live audience—boy, that wakes you up! Basically, the only sweetening you get on "Kelly & Company" is John and his infectious laugh. But John's laugh is great for a comedian. He'll start laughing and you think to yourself, "Man, I'm doing great."

That's important because when people in the audience come in to the studio and hear that a comedian is going to be on the show that day, they are already set in their minds, "This is going to be funny." In fact, I have even gone out to the hallway when the audience is assembling—before "Kelly & Company" opens up the studio—to do an impromptu warm-up. You want the audience to be as hot as possible.

For the nighttime talk shows like Carson and Griffin, I usually do stuff out of my act. On "The Tonight Show," and, to a lesser extent, on "The Merv Griffin Show," a talent coordinator will go over every joke beforehand. They don't do that after you've done the show enough. Then, they'll just ask you for your last joke so they'll know when to end the segment. You're usually on stage for a five- or six-minute routine, but if you're using material that you've used many times in a club, you can feel pretty comfortable knowing that most of it will work.

For a morning talk show like "Kelly & Company," there is an interview situation, usually with John because he seems to like to work with comedians. The producers will have briefed you first, to see what you've been doing, so the questions are right on. Sometime during the show, the producers will dream up something visual and comedic for me to do that involves the audience too. Not just a typical stand-up routine.

When I am being interviewed, I like to stay in character and be funny. I don't want to be thrown any curves and be asked what I think about Nicaragua. John understands what a comedian needs to maintain his public persona. He always asks the right questions and never throws me off.

Because Detroit is home, I usually try out some new material, or do a new song, whenever I am on the show. I remember my first appearance, October 1977. It was my first TV show, just before I made the move to California, and well before I had my role in the movie *Body Heat*. I had my guitar and I was going to sing one of my songs, "They Don't Make Nun Names [Like That No-More]." I had arranged beforehand with the technical director to play band tracks in the background for accompaniment.

Such a kick—your first TV show in your home town. I was absolutely catatonic!

But like I said, the producers take care of me. The production people in New York or Los Angeles are not any better than the ones who work in Detroit on Seven. They just happen to be in Detroit instead of L.A. or New York. One time the "Kelly & Company" crew came up with a toupee fashion show for my benefit. Actually, I thought I looked a lot like William Shatner by the time they finished with me.

That proved to be so successful that the producers decided to go for broke. A year or so later they came up with a theme show, a bald-headed extravaganza, in which all the segments were dedicated to the subject of baldness. Even the majority of the audience was bald. I saw my reflection many times over in those shiny domes. Was that ever strange!

Another time, a masseuse was on and I made a surprise entrance wearing nothing but a towel and a lot of oil. Like Orca, the beached whale.

Still another standout was a show they did on location at the Premiere Center. Everyone was dressed in tuxedos, and the producers arranged for me to rent one at Valente's when I arrived in town. Only they arranged for me to get the worst-looking outfit in the world, to see what I would do with it.

I decided to really put some thought into the right accessories for this number—so I came out barefoot! I figured that I would work the audience by trying to borrow some shoes from someone in the studio. Now, I wear a size eleven shoe, and I found one guy in the audience who was just furious with me for wanting to borrow his shoes. We did a little business with that, and he finally let me wear them. But he got the last word—he wore about a size eight!

I think it is an awful lot harder to be a host than a guest. You have to keep it going and keep it interesting. One time when I was hosting, the producers had arranged a punk-rock fashion show. I was wearing my Catholic school uniform, blue blazer, gray pants, white shirt, black shoes with laces. Now, I look like an AAA claims adjuster to begin with, so you already get a picture of what is going on.

Anyway, Zenobia X, a local punk rocker, and her boyfriend, Norm Dead, were featured as models. She was wearing your typical anti-Catholic outfit: black leather skirt, Nazi stockings, lots of black eye makeup. The nuns would have been hard at work scrubbing her face down with Borax if they had gotten a look at her in my neighborhood. For jewelry, she had some safety pins in her ears and two bracelets on her wrists, each with big spikes on them.

I was on the riser having some fun with that when one male model with a bleached blonde mohawk raced over and gave me an elbow right in the ribs, knocking me right off my feet and off the riser!

But these are just little inconveniences. I keep coming back because I know the producers will never let me die on "Kelly & Company." Even though they seem determined to give it their best shot.

RICHARD SIMMONS

When I began my career, I basically began in soap operas. The producers of "Kelly & Company" just called me, out of the blue, almost at the very beginning of the show. At that point in my career, I had not done a great deal of local talk shows or national talk shows.

I know I come out sounding kind of crazy, and when I first started doing their show, I was the lighthearted guest. It was fun, we laughed, and we exercised. But I've always had a great deal of interest in overweight women, the ones who have lost track of their lives. They realized that I wasn't just a lighthearted animated person. That I really busted my buns and I really do care. John is also concerned with the identity of human beings. So we have gotten into serious talk about obese women and all of the topics around it.

I think that is one of the reasons the "Kelly & Company" show is so popular. I guess you'd say they are the Waltons of morning talk shows. I mean, they are very "family," and they have started a lot of people's careers.

They helped my career. My book came out about a year after I started doing "Kelly & Company," and it helped me enormously in the Detroit area. Talk about loyalty! After I got my syndicated exercise show, they still had me on "Kelly & Company," even though I was on a different station in the same time slot!

It is very hard to go from local to national, not just in the world of television, but in anything. The reason "Kelly & Company" has not been syndicated is because they are goodie two shoes compared to a lot of talk shows, like "Donahue." With John and Marilyn, it is very hard to argue on subjects, and they don't "attack" the way a Donahue type of interview does. Besides, they do an awful lot of local stuff. Oprah Winfrey and Donahue do more national things. Maybe if John and Marilyn were to become bitchy to each other and be ugly and do exploitive topics, they would become syndicated. People like to watch a winner and a loser. But that's not what John and Marilyn stand for.

I just think, at the ripe old age of almost forty, I am very cynical about how I look at things. Do you know what the highest-rated competition is against "A.M. L.A.," the Los Angeles morning show? Bugs Bunny!

THOMAS HEARNS

"Kelly & Company" was my first appearance on television, back in 1979. I was a top-grade professional fighter then, working for the Kronk Organization, but I was not the champion. And I was very shy. Even the first couple of shows that I did were difficult. I felt myself freeze up, really become scared beforehand.

On the first show, I cooked breakfast for John. I've

been on probably about forty or fifty times since, sometimes even at the last minute when a scheduled guest can't make it from out of town. At first the producers would talk to me before the show and give me some idea of what was going to happen, but not now. Marilyn has done interviews with me, too. The only difference is that the questions are a little slower and I watch what I say a little more in front of a lady.

No two shows are ever the same, and I think I feel a whole lot more confident about doing live TV since all of these appearances. I've even done the Carson show, and I don't see any difference, except that "Kelly & Company" is in Detroit. I don't feel shy in front of the camera anymore. I even look forward to it, and I've been tested on the show. The audiences ask a lot of questions about everything, including my personal life. I've answered all their questions. I feel I've got nothing to hide. People ask what it's like to fight, what it feels like to be a champion? Sometimes I'll get some questions about how I train.

I got into boxing when I was nine years old. I started working out at a gym, not with the idea of making a career but to protect myself on the street. I had more than my share of fighting in the street. I was small and shy for my age besides.

You still have to protect yourself when you are a public figure. Gossip is something you have to learn to deal with. The press likes to print bad news and people love to read it, whether it is true or not. I've done a lot of fund-raising for the Detroit Public Library, for example. Personal appearances and all. I was pleased to help out, but the press criticized me, asking why didn't I raise more money. I got credit, but bad credit for it.

I find I still have to protect myself, mind my Ps

and Qs. But when there is a fight coming up, I feel that I need all of the press I can get.

TRISTAN ROGERS

There is never an ideal time to do a talk show. The timing is always bad. You just have to rise to the occasion. Working in California as I do, an appearance on "Kelly & Company" means you've been riding the "red-eye" all night, so you've got a good case of jet lag before you even get started. Usually there is just enough time to go to the hotel to change. You're hungry and tired, but you have to be ready to deliver on the air and be entertaining.

Doing a remote broadcast by satellite is no better. I've had to get up at four in the morning to appear by satellite on "Good Morning America."

However, a live audience can be a lot of fun. On a morning show, the tempo is a bit slower. You don't have to be quite so extroverted and as snappy with a reply as you do on "The Tonight Show," for example.

In a talk show, there are certain basic standbys that the producers can use to present a celebrity. Maybe the celebrity will show up with something timely, such as a film clip or a book. But this isn't the case for every celebrity. For morning shows, you usually rely on the producers to have something planned. "Kelly & Company" was always one of the better organized ones. They always know what you've been up to, so they'll be right on target with questions or situations.

When I was appearing as Scorpio in "General Hospital" and making the "regular" rounds of the talk shows, I would get shut right off when I was being interviewed by someone who hadn't seen the show. The questions get very thin very quickly in that circumstance.

For me, my interest in auto racing is a good hook to talk about in a morning show, especially one in Detroit. I made an appearance on "Kelly & Company" in 1983 when I was driving in the Detroit Grand Prix sponsored by American Motors Corporation. I made another appearance on the show in conjunction wth the 1985 race, even though I wasn't driving in that one.

All told, I have done the show three or four times, but the producers frequently invite me to come back. I've been on when John and Marilyn have come to California to do the shows and we worked together for two days on "General Hospital" when John and Marilyn made a two-day guest appearance.

"Kelly & Company" has always presented me in a positive light, but I always try to get a general idea beforehand from the producers as to what they have in mind for me to do. If talk shows can keep their ratings up by making you look bad or foolish, they'll do it.

JOHN

We've appeared on "All My Children" and, a couple of years ago, on "General Hospital." Both were fun experiences—absolutely. I prefer not to discuss "All My Children," mainly because Marilyn was given a juicy part, while I was a grunting nerd sitting next to her. (Come to think of it, it wasn't much better on "General Hospital.") The roles on "All My Children" were of a talk show couple (strange!) questioning Erica Kane (Susan Lucci). Well, actually Marilyn did the questioning (the script said so) while I just—as I said—grunted. Terrific. The director fell in love with Marilyn's face and expression, and wound up the scene cutting back and forth between extreme close-ups of Marilyn and Susan.

A year or so later, we were on the set of "General Hospital." Our scenes were with Scorpio (Tristan Rogers) and Emma Samms, who played his wife and ace assistant, as they were on the track of a couple of bad guys. The scene was in the terminal building of the West Palm Beach, Florida, airport. I was an airline agent, while Marilyn was a car rental clerk. Fate struck again (or maybe good taste) and Marilyn was given two scenes with the detectives. I was given one. A short one. All I had to do was look at a photo Scorpio handed me, tell him I couldn't identify the guy because it was so busy at that time, and that was it. I blew it sky high in rehearsal. Of course, they were carrying their scripts, which made me feel a little better. Marilyn had her lines locked—for both scenes.

It took an entire day. Not just for us, but for the shooting of an entire episode. We showed up early as we were supposed to. "General Hospital" is shot in what ABC calls "Gower Street," meaning the studios, part of the old Columbia Pictures lot, located on Gower Street. A sound stage has been converted for daily television videotape production. The basement area consists of offices, dressing rooms for the regulars, makeup department, wardrobe, and various others. There is also a very large green room, which is sort of a pleasant waiting room that the stars and regulars can use if they wish, and which the day players and extras must use when they're not in makeup or wardrobe or standing at a hallway pay phone calling their agents to see where the next job is, or if there is one.

Marilyn and I were given dressing rooms fairly

close to each other, rooms belonging to actors who were not working that day. In New York, a large rehearsal hall was used for the read-through and blocking, with folding chairs filling in as doors, tables, couches, lamps, closets—whatever the scene called for. In L.A., or at least on "General Hospital," rehearsal was on the set, even if it was not finished and yet to be lighted. So for the first run-through, there we were, sitting nervously in our dressing rooms reading lines, moving into the green room for coffee, and then back to our dressing rooms.

Finally, a quiet public address system paged us and the stars to the set, and we went like a pair of bullets. Nervous? Absolutely. Afterward, we were taken to wardrobe where we were fitted in our costumes . . . which, in our case, were uniforms. I sort of liked mine . . . blue blazer, gray slacks, black socks, shoes, white shirt, and dark red tie. The blazer had a thin red stripe near the cuff . . . it really did look like those outfits passenger agents wear. Marilyn was not too thrilled with hers but was too excited to really care.

About this time came a break for lunch, which we grabbed off a catering wagon in the parking lot. We then learned that they had just started shooting a show called "Mr. Belvedere" in the next sound stage, and the rumor was that it was for a fall start on ABC. Afterward, dress rehearsal, and then for both of us, a trip to makeup, and for Marilyn, a hair stylist or, as they call it out there, "hair."

At about three in the afternoon on the set, the scenes were shot. There was one retake, and that was it. Tristan and Emma of course were perfect. Marilyn was perfect. Me—well, let's say I was involved in the one retake. Then, it was over.

Before we went there, we'd heard all the stories

about temper tantrums and cocaine and bad boys and naughty girls on the "General Hospital" set, but everyone was delightful. The production people—director, stage manager, stagehands—all of them were patient and friendly. Emma and Tristan were not only quite professional on the set, but very friendly throughout. The makeup artists—all women at the time—were beyond helpful, they were wonderful. So were the wardrobe ladies. They were floored when I, in my ignorance, came trotting back to them with my costume after we were finished. They usually went to the actors' dressing rooms and picked costumes up at the end of the day.

Late in the afternoon, producer Jill Coughlin, who had accompanied us to L.A., and Marilyn and I set up our own camera crew and shot interviews that we used later on "Good Afternoon Detroit." Again, full cooperation from all of them, Tristan, Emma, and Jackie Zeman, who plays Bobbie Spencer.

About the only sour note was when Jill tried to line up Jack Wagner (Frisco) and the woman who played his heartthrob, Felicia. They just couldn't be bothered, they said; they had other things to do. Jill, to her undying credit, gazed at them and said, "Who needs you?" and walked away. About ten minutes later they came along, and it turned out they had time for us after all. Surprise.

We'd like to do it again, and probably will.

JEFFREY BRUCE

Nancy Lenzen loves to have me on the show during ratings weeks because she says I bring in a good-looking audience. I feel that Nancy had a part in discovering me, or at least my potential for television, and she has an unerringly good sense of what is right for the show.

Fashion and beauty are right—they are important components in any day-time talk show that will have a largely female viewing audience. Besides, I am outrageous on the air. I'll do anything and I don't take myself very seriously. I mean, I hosted a mother-infant show once for "Kelly & Company," where we just had mothers and kids under eighteen months comprising the whole audience. I spent the whole ninety minutes dressed in a beautiful new three-piece suit and bib!

My first encounter with "Kelly & Company" came in a roundabout way, via Atlantic City, in 1980. I was there to do the makeup for Heidi Heppler, the Michigan entry for the Miss America pageant that year. Heidi's mother said that there was a need for someone like me in the Detroit area.

I said, "That's very nice, thank you, but how are people going to find out about me?" She said that if I wanted to come to Detroit to do makeovers and work up a clientele, she would arrange for me to appear on "Kelly & Company," the Number One local talk show.

She did get me on—for one brief segment—without any demonstrations. The first thing I said to Marilyn when I came on was, "What's with the bangs?" She asked what I meant, and I replied, "Either you're too old for them or they are too young for you!"

I didn't know who she was, had never met her before. But I wasn't intimidated by her in the least. And to give you an idea of the power of the show, I had six solid months of appointments booked in the Detroit area after that appearance.

I have lost track of how many times I have done

the show, both as a guest and as a substitute host, at least twenty-five times. There are about fourteen daytime talk shows that I do on a regular basis, appearing once about every six weeks on each of them, including shows in New York, Tampa, St. Louis, Baltimore, and Pittsburgh, but "Kelly & Company" was the first, and that has been my longest association. And Detroit has been a great city. I can never understand why Detroiters are so negative and critical about their city.

The first time Nancy Lenzen called to ask me to be a substitute host after having done many guest shots, I thought she was kidding. I had never hosted a TV show in my life.

I started right in without a safety net that first show. No opening patter—I just went right into introducing my very first guest, a writer named Alexandra Penney, who was promoting her book, *How to Make Love to a Man*. To do this tome, she had interviewed more than 200 men about what they like most about sex.

"Please welcome Alexandra Penney to 'Kelly & Company' [applause, applause]. I am so happy to see you, Alexandra. You're not as bowlegged as I thought you'd be."

It set the whole tone for the show, and Jeanne Findlater loved it. I love Jeanne, I really do. Jeanne makes me laugh. But I know that I have gotten her nose out of joint a few times. She usually says, "Oh that Jeffrey, he can be such a bad boy!" when my name comes up.

At one point, I was scheduled to appear right after a recent appearance by Polly Bergen, who had been in Detroit to promote a new line of Polly Bergen shoes. Now, the show is very sensitive to commercialism. And there are some hard-and-fast rules on this.

As hosts, we tell all of the guests that the host, not the guest, promotes or mentions the book or product. We show the product, whether it be a book, movie, or whatever, at the beginning and at the end of the segment. If the guest makes mention of it and starts hyping in any way, we break to a commercial. Or we can make a light joke out of it, but the guest will *not* be asked back again.

Polly Bergen managed to push everything in sight during her segment. John admired her ring, and she said, "I'm glad you like it. It's from my new line of Polly Bergen costume jewelry." I think for twenty-five cents, she would license her mother! Anyhow, I came on for my segment and I said to Marilyn, "Do you like my new tuxedo? It's my new Polly Bergen tuxedo. Do you like my nose job? It's a Polly Bergen nose job." Marilyn—and the audience—were screaming.

There have been many good things that have come out of my association with "Kelly & Company." Some people might think there is competition between the three of us. Not so. John and Marilyn are both very basic, and have been good friends to me as well as good professionals to work with. Two years ago, someone from the Nederlander Organization called and asked me if I wanted to appear at the Birmingham Theatre for a role in a revival of *A Funny Thing Happened on the Way to the Forum*. It was a momentous event for me, my first shot at an acting role—and John, Marilyn, and Dean came opening night and stood up in the audience to lead the applause at the end of the performance.

11
FEEDBACK

THE PRODUCERS

BRAD

What is producing? I get asked that question a lot.
It's more than writing. We do a lot of writing in
connection with the show. But producing is more
than just typing a script.

That first glimmer of an idea is producing. And so
are the last details. We take care of myriad details,
flight arrangements for the guests, even deciding
who is or who is not going to be an interesting guest.
You can have the most exciting topic in the world,
but if you can't find somebody who is "good television," it will not come across.

Basically, producing is coordinating. It's putting
everything into twenty minutes, thinking it out, even
seeing it inside your head, with guests, props, ques-

tions, the works. Because it has to be visual, we have Lisa, our assistant, in charge of tracking down old tapes. Sometimes it will take weeks to put a segment together, but we've done segments in twenty-four hours when we've had to. Especially if someone cancels out.

What do we do when that happens? Well, we have a few regulars who help us out. Shirley Eder, stir-fry chef Maria Ang, TV trivia expert Gary Warner, and local attorney Harriet Rotter are some people we have called at the last minute.

Then, there are people who have let us down whom we will not call again, ever. Aretha Franklin is one. A lot of people wonder why we don't have her on the show. After all, she is right here in Detroit and has a tremendous following. We had her all set for a show and she stood us up once, so we will not book her again.

CARNELL

Basically we use our own curiosity to guide us. We are a team. How else could it be when we work up to ten hours each day together? The four of us are all different personalities and come from different backgrounds, but if it is a topic that we are interested in, we think the audience will be, too. We rely on letters and phone calls from some of our "regulars." Nancy has her "fat lady," for example, who called one day and suggested the idea for our "fat show."

JILL

And we're not all penis and vagina either. Many of our medical shows have been informative and important and help a lot of people. Our audience is basically women, ages twenty-five to fifty-nine, and we target our topics to them. But that can be a lot broader a range than you think. Our show on penile implants, for example, though male-oriented, is a subject that affects everyone. The partner may blame herself for the problem. So there's a topic that will touch a broad range of viewers, no matter who is watching out there.

We don't mind the sensational, but we don't want to be exploitive. It's a fine line. I've wanted to do a show on leprosy for a long time. I've located some cooperative lepers. So far Nancy has said a definite *no*.

NANCY

We have had circus sideshow acts appear as guests, but I don't see that as exploitive. After all, appearing in public is how these people make their living. There was one instance that caused a lot of debate over whether we were being exploitive, but I felt it was an important and touching show. In 1982, we had a pair of Siamese twins, joined at the head, and their mother.

They were traveling around the country trying to raise money. The mother was old and ill and was worried about how these girls would get along after she died. I suppose you could accuse her of exploitation, but she didn't want them to be reduced to performing in a circus.

The twins were in their mid-twenties and were wonderful. They answered every question, including things like "How do you go to the bathroom?" and "How do you go on dates?" It was so sad, though. Marilyn did the interview and asked the mother what she wanted for her daughters. She said she wasn't going to be here forever, that they had a right to live, just like any other human being. Then the mother started to cry, Marilyn started to cry, the audience started to cry. Every woman could identify with the feeling—what if this happened to me? It was so moving that, at that moment in time, I do *not* think we could have been accused of exploitation.

The men at the station seemed to have more trouble with that show. Some of them told me later that they turned their sets off in the middle of it.

I have a simple analogy that I use frequently when I've given guest lectures to TV and communications students. A TV show is like the human body. The cameramen are the eyes, the audio men are the ears, John and Marilyn are the face and hands of the show. Our director, Mason Weaver, directs the nervous system and the heart that keeps it all pumping. And behind all that, to make it think and work, is the brain, and that's the producers.

I began working in television on the old Lou Gordon show. Not as a producer, not even as an assistant or a researcher, but as a secretary. I had been a teacher before I left to raise my four children. When I went back to take it up again, I found that my credentials had expired and I needed to go back to school. I started applying for jobs, and I heard about the opening on the Lou Gordon show. That experience provided me with a rare opportunity to learn from the ground up. I met Bob Woodruff, who was producing, and soon moved up to become his researcher.

Because we are a local show, I think we have a lot more latitude in our subject matter than a network show. Donahue has had several important shows that have been censored. I am thinking of one on a live home birth that several stations wouldn't air. We have never had that problem. We can judge our audience reaction by what they call about, or write, or say in the studio. I think one of the best questions that ever came from our audience was during a show with two lesbians who were raising a family. They stimulated many questions such as, "Do your parents approve?" and "Do you go to church?"

Finally one woman got up and said, "I've been listening to you two for I don't know how long. But tell me, what exactly is it that you do and how do you do it anyway?"

THE MAILBAG

JOHN

By now I'm sure you've heard the story of "Cagney and Lacey," and how a letter-writing campaign saved the show a few years ago when it appeared CBS had canceled it. It's true, and it shows how important television considers written and telephone response to be. It's also true at "Kelly & Company." Mail is obviously important in the infrequent contests we run. But it is also important to give an indication of what viewers are thinking. What they like, what they don't like. Who would they like to see, what they hated even though they felt it was important that it be shown. We read it all.

Well, almost all—nothing unsigned gets read, at least not by Marilyn or me. It's a personal policy I started years ago and which Marilyn adopted. Some of what we receive is pure, unreasoning hate. If it's unsigned, we consider it trash, and we simply don't want to be bothered with it. Why should we? We can't respond. So why bother? The hate mail that contains a name and address, however, we answer.

We even have special letterheads for answering our viewers. Marilyn is much better at that than I am. I'm not much of a letter writer.

Some letters are so interesting or provocative that we save them and on occasion use them on the air, without revealing the names of the writers.

To Whom It May Concern:

I was on your "Kelly & Company" Show 7/3 of last year regarding my husband's suicide. I wanted to take the opportunity to let you know how much my visit to your show helped me. I just recently went through a second suicide, my father. My visit on your show helped me meet others that I could turn to. . . .

You there at "Kelly & Company" helped me so much that I would like to return the favor. If at sometime you would like to do a spot on suicides again, I'd be more than willing to come in and help in any way possible. . . .

Thank you very much again,
Mrs. D.C., Oak Park, MI

Dear Sir or Madam:

With my morning ritual of watching "Kelly & Company" and my cup of coffee in hand I couldn't believe what I was hearing coming out of the mouth of that paralyzed victim of domestic violence, Diana Davis. I can't imagine where her head is at—or maybe I can. That is—possible book, TV, movie, or celebrity status on "Kelly & Company" or "Donahue" (sorry about that). . . .

I, being the mother of a murder victim, who was killed by a mentally ill but guilty person who killed his mother and father and then hid his father's body

*in the family freezer, strangled his pet cat, also
killed his brother-in-law, another person who was
an aquaintance, and wounded two others in California prior to coming to Michigan for this ram-
page, pray that Diana Davis pauses and thinks of
what could happen if her husband is released from
prison.*

*I pray that people don't think that she represents
the majority of victims.*

    Sincerely,
    L.S., Westland, MI

Dear Kelly & Company:
 *. . . I am writing to suggest that you interview
staff, kids, and perhaps parents connected with
Straight, Inc., a drug rehabilitation program located in Plymouth, Michigan.*

*My daughter graduated from Straight 20 months
ago. She is doing wonderful things for herself. . . .*

*I hope you will consider this for a future
interview.*

    Sincerely
    S.T., Ann Arbor, MI

Dear Mr. & Mrs. Kelly:
 *It is with a touch of sadness and regret that I write
this letter to you this day. . . . You and your program
have taken such a disappointing plunge. I refer to
your guest of this day, the stripper from Jason's.
Really, are you running so short of entertainment
that you have to resort to the dregs of humanity and
shove it down our throats? . . .*

*Do you really think that anyone is interested in
the life of a stripper and do you feel such a person
deserves the prestige of appearing on your show?*

You are, in effect, putting your stamp of approval on strippers. . . . I find it very hard to make any kind of excuse for anyone resorting to stripping for a living. This person is exploiting the female and putting her up there for men who have nothing better to do, to ogle: and you, Marilyn, approve of this and are helping her. Shame on you!

> *Very sincerely*
> *Some former viewers from*
> *Windsor, N.H., C.C., J.B.*

Dear Marilyn & John:

We are here in Las Vegas with a group of seniors, and my wife, Ruth, and I are on our second honeymoon. We want to thank "Kelly & Company" for the wonderful and truly inspiring show "60 and Over" that you aired recently.

All of us got a heap of inspiration out of it, and the gang of nurses and patients at Oakwood Hospital were thrilled with the concept that older people should work at good health and good spirits.

> *Yours sincerely,*
> *R. & R. C., The Charleston*
> *Champ, almost 80 years young*

Dear Mr. Weaver:

I understand you determine what people appear as guests on "Kelly & Company." I enjoy the show, but I am getting sick and tired of having someone talking about sex almost every day. Sex is overdone on TV completely, and I am getting sick of it.

> *Sincerely,*
> *Mrs. M.S., Warren, MI*

To Whoever Is Responsible for Programming "Kelly & Company":

I feel that you are scraping the bottom of the barrel for guests. Your show with Anita Bryant was the only bright light this week. CLEAN UP YOUR PROGRAM. SEX, SEX, SEX. I am 67 years old and had a beautiful marriage, but sex was only a minor part of it. . . .

. . . I really believe that even John and Marilyn were embarrassed by the show when you had those two sick gays on.

> *A Disgusted Listener,*
> *I.S., Brighton   R.S.V.P.*

Dear Kelly & Company!

What a super program!! My son, aged 3, and I watched the program with the live birth. What an experience!

My son was born C-section and being totally put under, I did not see him being born. . . . I cried when I saw Karen coming out. What a great time. My son asked all kinds of questions, which to me was O.K.

> *Thanks again for a wonderful program*
> *Mrs. P.H. and Timmy, Flint*

Dear Kelly & Company:

John Kelly, you deserve a truckload of roses. How in the world did you keep that Irish temper down when you interviewed those two #π%*&! on Thursday's program?

It made me sick to hear about man-boy love, but I congratulate Channel 7 for airing this program. I am 56 and a grandmother of ten. I believe in hugging my babies—not masturbating them for pleasure.

> *Sincerely,*
> *S.P., Westland*

189

HARVEY GERSIN

Television is an intimate medium, and people watch it for many reasons that transcend the issues of content and personality or talent. For some people who are social, like to join groups, and be "in-the-know," TV teaches them interesting things that they can tell to others, and that can make them feel important in their own minds. Self-respect is important for all of us. Viewers can watch a talk show, learn something interesting, share it with others, and feel good about themselves.

For some viewers who do not go out much or travel, TV brings the world in and fills the loneliness. The psychology gets more complex here. The personalities on the tube are intimate to them, like their family or friends.

Although viewers don't want to see plastic people whom they can't identify with, these people on TV are viewed as authority figures who have achieved a certain position in life. In other words, their sentiments are not necessarily all black or white. Viewers may watch talk show hosts or news anchors because they love them—or because they envy or hate them—or all the shades of gray in between.

12
EQUAL TIME

THE SIREN SONG OF SYNDICATION

MARILYN

Syndication is the beckoning finger to every successful local show like "Kelly & Company." Most shows
begin as locals. "The Oprah Winfrey Show" was a
local show in Chicago. "Donahue," as most know,
started as a local show in Dayton, Ohio. As far as *our*
show is concerned, we were told by various people
outside the station for years that we should be in
syndication. The ratings track record seemed to
emphasize that. ABC and our station management
showed no interest until 1982, when they began to
negotiate a new contract with us that would cover
not only "Kelly & Company" but also "Good Afternoon Detroit," which was a new concept in local
programming. Jeanne Findlater and Phil Boyer—at
that time special assistant to the president of the

ABC-owned stations, Dick O'Leary—flew to our vacation spot in Florida to discuss the show and the proposition. At that time, and in subsequent negotiations with our attorney, Henry Baskin, the subject of syndication for "Kelly & Company" kept coming up. Ultimately, Phil promised (and wrote into the contract) that a major presentation to blue chip syndicators would be made annually in New York. We were present for one, and we know of another that was made. From one of them came the deal with 20th Century-Fox. WXYZ was always lukewarm on the idea. The expense for start-up (estimated at that time at about $25,000 minimum) was one reason, another was concern for the *local* aspect of the show. All of that became academic when both ABC and Fox were sold. Potential buyers dried up, even though the show had been placed in some markets like Indianapolis and Palm Beach. To our knowledge, no major New York presentations have been made since that time.

JOHN

"Good Afternoon Detroit" originated in the ABC headquarters in New York. It was the brainchild of Dick O'Leary, the then president of the Owned and Operated Stations Division. Marilyn and I were vacationing in Florida one hot summer when we were visited by Dick's right-hand man, Phil Boyer, and Jeanne Findlater. They explained to us the concept of the show and said that research indicated we were the ones for the show. A new contract was negotiated for us.

"Good Afternoon Detroit" was a big-bucks show. The set was designed by Rene Laglar, who designs for Sinatra specials and whose latest project was the

192

set for the Sunday night spectacular during the Liberty Weekend on ABC on the Fourth of July. Tens of thousands of dollars were spent on the set.

The show was planned and designed by Bob and Ann Shanks. He has written a number of books on the business and planned the new "Good Morning America." They spent a couple of months in Detroit, hiring staff, approving talent, and working with the management (with whom they did not get along).

The staff was more than fifty people. We had our own camera crews for the field, our own separate editing space, and our own newly built office. Dick O'Leary hinted that it would be a national show soon after its start, with Marilyn and I acting as hosts in Detroit, feeding the show to all owned and operated stations in New York, Chicago, Los Angeles, and San Francisco. Each of the participating cities would in turn feed its features to us.

Needless to say, it never got off the ground as a national show. The other stations resisted the idea, feeling they should be able to do their own show.

Meanwhile, "Good Afternoon Detroit" remained "Good Afternoon Detroit" instead of becoming "Good Afternoon America," and we plugged along. It was successful, for a long time Number One in its timeslot. However, about a year prior to the sale of WXYZ to Scripps Howard, the cutbacks began as *economy* became the ABC byword. Apparently the cuts were not enough for Scripps. Six months after taking over, they canceled the show after a nearly four-year run.

MARILYN

Why do we want syndication? A lot of reasons. A secured future is one of them. Another is ambition, pure and simple. We really believe (and so did 20th Century-Fox) there is a market for our kind of program. As of this writing, nowhere out there can there be found a daytime talk-entertainment-variety program. Inside the business, with agents, authors, stars, we have an outstanding reputation. Given the opportunity, we know it can be done. We want to do it—and we want to do it from Detroit. What a wonderful thing for this city!

JEANNE FINDLATER

Could "Kelly & Company" "make it" in New York or Los Angeles?

Not without changes. There are regional differences in programming. I have studied the KABC morning talk show in Los Angeles and there is a difference. They do things that would not work in the same way in Detroit. I remember a few years ago when the KABC program did a series of cooking segments that devoted an entire week to tofu cookery. Tofu became popular in Michigan years later, and even when it did, I don't think our viewers would relish a whole week of it.

But to suggest that this kind of regionalism dominates TV program directors' selections is wrong, because I believe that television has shortened the distances in our country and in our cultural patterns over the past ten years.

There is instant communication today, largely because of television. A fad like the hula hoop that used to take four to six weeks to get across the country can spread across the country in a day.

MIKE DUFFY

Will it play? Donahue started out in Dayton, middle

America, and then went to Chicago. Another major talk show host of the sixties, Mike Douglas, started out in Cleveland when Group W picked him up for national syndication. But I think the "The Mike Douglas Show" was a 1960s phenomenon. I don't think a show that "homey" could work that way again. There is much more pressure to succeed quickly on the air these days. Both Douglas and Donahue were on the air a long time before they gained national numbers.

And there is the issue of personality and regionalism. There are some news anchors who have had trouble translating their personalities and charisma from one market to another. Look at Bill Bonds, a Babe Ruth of newscasters in Detroit. But he never cut it in New York or Los Angeles. Why? It's not because he is not a good anchorperson. Maybe the mix isn't right. The person sitting next to him doesn't click for the right chemistry. The point is, you can't just pick up a Bill Bonds from one market and put him into another and be sure it will work the same way.

My own feeling is that John and Marilyn probably could make a go of their show nationally, but it is a question of how they want to do it.

JOHN

In 1972, just after I was hired on at WXYZ-TV, and while this show tentatively called "Kelly & Company" was in the planning stages, I was invited to lunch by a guy with Grey Advertising. (They were still in Detroit then, and had the WXYZ account.) We settled in at our table and ordered a drink. He ruffled his eyebrows, lit a cigarette, and planted his elbows on the table; then he leaned toward me with a confidential air and asked, "What is your philosophy for this show?"

Philosophy! Hell, my philosophy was to earn the salary that was nearly double what I was making at Channel Two, work with the producer, and have a good time by doing the best I could. When I told him that, he was not amused. The luncheon was downhill from there, and I was glad when it ended.

That show lasted less than six months before I was back doing the news again. But I've thought about that remark off and on since then. It really comes down to three words: variety, information, entertainment. Probably entertainment would cover it all. We Americans have let the word come to mean one-liners, pratfalls, and belly laughs. But, of course, it means much more. To entertain does not necessarily mean to amuse. Not to me. Not to us. It means to grab and hold the viewers' attention. We tell them something they didn't know or remind them of something they'd forgotten. We warn them of danger, or help them get better, or point them in a direction, or give them a good feeling and even make them nostalgic.

To try to give a history of our show after eight years is difficult. Record-keeping requires a big staff. We don't have one. It requires a massive archive system. We don't have one. It requires keeping a tape of every show. Tapes are much too expensive. Besides, nobody ever gave that more than a passing thought.

But we do have our memories.

Like the time Marilyn was making a promotional announcement for the King of the Hobos—only she called him King of the Homos. Or the time we were horrified to learn Marilyn had to interview Siamese twins—young ladies joined at the head. It became one of the most heartrending yet tender and revealing programs we have ever done—a presentation of love and hope.

196

Or Sea World of Ohio. For three years straight we took all of "Kelly & Company" to Aurora, Ohio (just outside Cleveland), and invited a few thousand of our audience to join us, giving entire families free tickets. They were marvelous shows. Sea World really is family entertainment at its best. Marilyn water-skied and was part of a skiers flag-carrying pyramid, riding on a man's shoulders. I took part in a grand chase and shootout in a western town with a gang of Hollywood stuntmen. We had shows with the dolphins and the killer whales and were half-drowned when our then-producer, Dan Weaver, plotted with the Sea World folks to have the whales soar from the water and fall back, splashing us with a ton of water! I donned a wetsuit and entered the walrus pool, dancing with one of them. And through it all, thousands of our people from the Detroit area were there—entire families laughing and applauding. And later we learned through cards, letters, calls, and personal encounters that for many of them it was their only summer vacation that year.

And there was the young woman suffering from agoraphobia—the fear of leaving her home. She couldn't even walk to the corner drugstore without being overcome by a pounding, heartstopping, choking fear. So we took a camera into her home. I stayed in the studio and talked with her through a TV set next to me. It was searing in its simple yet painful message. At the end—and to this day I don't know where it came from—I told her that I was expecting her to show up in our studio audience one day to give me a hug. A year later, she did.

Shows that we call specials, theme shows in other words, were devoted to the fifties. We did several specials on country music. Who can forget "Goober" from the old "Andy Griffith" show spitting watermelon seeds into a tub from twenty feet away? And then the seniors—all people over sixty who danced in a chorus line like the Radio City Rockettes—or roller-skated every day, outdoing much younger people. They were inspiring.

Often in our mail we find letters complaining about too much sex. We've had homosexuals, transsexuals, transvestites, and androgynous men. For instance, there was a man who liked to dress like a woman, complete with makeup, pantyhose, and fine wig. He showed up in full feminine attire, with his wife and two children. We asked the children what they thought of it, and to the parents' surprise, the son said he didn't like it at all, that it bothered him a great deal.

Then there was the young man who submitted to long, painful, and repeated surgery to become a woman physically as well as psychologically. When it was all over, he found it had been a lousy idea—and he was in the midst of trying to change back again. Unbelievable—but certainly thought-provoking.

MARILYN

I have tons of pictures, storage boxes full, that I have carted around with me through the years, each time I have moved. It seems as though I have sifted through thousands of them to prepare for this book. I cannot believe the number that have been taken through the years—how they have encompassed so many different aspects of my life. Family, children, husbands, career—they are all there—frozen in time.

Some date back to my earliest days in Detroit, in front of the weather board at Channel Two, the rough-and-ready days of local television. There is a beautiful glossy copy of my first publicity photo for Channel Seven that had the caption "Marilyn Turner, you're our kind of girl!"

Bob Turner and I were picture takers—there are snapshots, millions of snapshots, from those years. I had some storage boxes stolen years ago, when I lived in Regency Square near downtown Detroit, after my divorce from Bob. They contained many photos from the early family years when my sons were small, but we had also taken many rolls of movie film. About five years ago I spent an entire weekend holed up inside the house going through those old films. I condensed about eighty reels into eight. Even so, there is still a wealth of candids to sort through, probably a suitcase full of snapshots showing my relationship with John, and our personal pictures now.

Yet, there are other photos, important moments in my life, that are missing. I have no traces of commercial photos that I have posed in.

I know that I had a wonderful picture from my ice skating days, just four girls posing on a Windsor ice rink wearing big smiles, mittens on our hands, and short skating costumes, but I can't find it anywhere.

I stopped short of the storage boxes containing my wedding pictures from my marriage to Bob Turner. I have them—but I just didn't want to go through them.

And I was surprised that the most recent picture of me with my two sons was taken eight years ago. Rob lives in Florida, and Dean lives in Michigan, so we are seldom all together at the same time anymore.

I have many favorite photos hanging in my office at the station, and they show "special" moments in my career. At home that isn't the case. In my den and in the hall of our apartment, I have a collection of

photos of Marilyn Monroe. I have collected everything I have been able to get my hands on, even some
rare ones that have never been published in books or
magazines. John has had some of them matted and
framed for me, including a two-foot by three-foot
poster-sized one in the entry hall.

But that isn't my favorite. Several years ago, I
found one during one of our week-long "location"
trips to Los Angeles for "Kelly & Company." I had
been rummaging in a junky little shop that most
people wouldn't even know about when I found it.
She is standing in the ocean, the water coming
around her ankles, wearing just a pair of red shorts
and a blue T-shirt. She is smiling and hugging
herself, and she looks so innocent and so sweet. I
always have thought of her as a very pretty person, a
vulnerable person. Not as a sex symbol.

We have tapes of "Kelly & Company" too, although we never play them. The two weeks that the
show goes into reruns, I can hardly sit still and watch
for ten minutes. It's like yesterday's news. I've observed this phenomenon with our guests, too. Often
actors and movie stars who appear on "Kelly &
Company" with clips to plug a movie turn away
from the monitor when we show the film.

Why do I keep the tapes? Well, I expect to be able
to show them to my future grandchildren one day. If
I simply tried to tell them all of this, they might not
quite believe it.

JOHN

I've been involved in Detroit television for over
twenty-one years. Anchorman, reporter, talk show
host, and all of those one-time-only things that come
your way. And I'll tell you this: the people of this

city are the best. Detroit audiences, once they accept you, are loyal beyond all expectations. We get love letters, hate letters, death threats, handmade gifts, pictures, snapshots, paintings, caps, and even clothing. Twice we've had threats serious enough to warrant investigation—the bad guy was caught. We've been the target of a death threat that was to take place while we announced the 1985 Thanksgiving Day Parade. The Detroit Police Department learned of it and stuck to us like glue, door to door and back again.

It's a large part of one's life to use up, but it's what everyone does who works for a living. And despite the glamour associated with it from time to time, it is work. Would I trade it in? Not a minute of it! I'll probably bore the grandchildren someday, but thanks to Marilyn, we've got the videotape to prove it.

Reality, of course, is being dead-tired at the end of a day. Remember that foggy early, *early* morning I wrote of at the beginning of this book? That's usually preceded by trying to get to bed early the night before. I have to read myself to sleep. Marilyn, believe it or not, uses television to do the same thing, and it works in minutes.

We miss some things by living the schedule we do, but eight years, ninety minutes a day, five times a week, Marilyn and I have had an opportunity to visit places we never would have seen, do things we wouldn't normally think of trying, know people we never would have met, and, most important, feel things we never would have felt.

It's been a blast.

. . . we'll be right back.